THE TEACHER
AND STUDENT IN
LITERATURE

THE TEACHER AND STUDENT IN LITERATURE

A Literature Study and Creative Writing Course
to TAKE or to TEACH
as a Distance-Learning Student
or as a Real but Remote Instructor

ROBERT EIDELBERG

A Book With a Built-in Teacher

This Book With a Built-in Teacher is not a work of fiction. It is, in effect, a textbook example of the special topics courses offered by the English Department of Hunter College of the City University of New York. As its subtitle indicates, this "education-in-literary-fiction" book is presented for any intrigued student to *take on their own* and for any interested secondary school or college instructor to *teach as their own*.

Cover Design by Robert Eidelberg

Contact author Robert Eidelberg and, through him, any of his sixteen student collaborators at: glamor62945@mypacks.net

Print information available on the last page.

Rev. date: 05/25/2021

These twenty-eight scheduled and seven bonus sessions of literature study and creative writing lessons were taught In the fall semester of Pandemic 2020 by the real but remote Professor Robert Eidelberg to the following class act of sixteen distance-learning Hunter College undergraduate students whose imaginative and academic pieces of writing can be found throughout the pages of the education-in-fiction course you are about to take or to teach.

Anika Bradley
Rifath Islam
Destiny Bolding
Shelly Uzagir
Martin Ljuljduraj
Victoria Cecere
Janel Fernandez
Mahajabin Chowdhury
Jessica Chu
Khadiza Sultana
Hudaiba Khatri
Lisa Baez
Dixiory Burgos Utate
Jessica Ulloa
Jasmine Baird
Danny Jiang

"Teach me, I forget;
show me, I remember;
involve me, I understand"

This book is dedicated to true teachers and students,
actual and fictional

SCHEDULE OF CLASS SESSIONS

Welcome to the Email Correspondence Course Book for the
Study of The Teacher and Student in Literature......................................xiii

Colleague Profile / English 25147 The Teacher and Student in
Literature / Mr. Eidelberg / Fall 2020.. xv

Introductory Session #1 of The Teacher and Student in
Literature, and the Walt Whitman Poem "When I Heard the
Learn'd Astronomer"... 1

Session #2 of The Teacher and Student in Literature on
Remarkable, Albeit Fictional, Teachers 6

Session #3 of The Teacher and Student in Literature on Who's
the Teacher, Who's the Student, and Leo Tolstoy's 1886 short
story "The Three Hermits" 8

Session #4 of The Teacher and Student in Literature on "Help
Wanted, New Teacher Needed," and Miss Read's 1955 Novel
VILLAGE SCHOOL... 19

Session #5 of The Teacher and Student In Literature: "Covering"
Evan Hunter's 1954 Novel THE BLACKBOARD JUNGLE...................... 25

Session #6 of The Teacher and Student In Literature on Part
One of THE BLACKBOARD JUNGLE 27

Session #7 of The Teacher and Student In Literature on Part
Two of THE BLACKBOARD JUNGLE 29

Session #8 of The Teacher and Student In Literature on Part
Three of THE BLACKBOARD JUNGLE.. 31

Session #9 of The Teacher and Student In Literature on Remarkable Teaching and Learning in Evan Hunter's Novel THE BLACKBOARD JUNGLE 35

Session #10 of The Teacher and Student In Literature on the 1955 Hollywood Movie Version of Evan Hunter's Novel THE BLACKBOARD JUNGLE 39

Session #11 of The Teacher and Student in Literature on the 1967 film "To Sir, With Love" and Whether It Is a British "Blackboard Jungle" 44

Bonus Session of The Teacher and Student in Literature on Mind Games Students and Teachers Play 49

Session #12 of The Teacher and Student in Literature on Frank McCourt's 2004 Memoir TEACHER MAN 53

Session #13 of The Teacher and Student in Literature on the Tone of the Two-Word Title TEACHER MAN 56

Session #14 of The Teacher and Student in Literature: Hello to the 1934 Novella GOODBYE, MR. CHIPS 59

Session #15 of The Teacher and Student in Literature on James Hilton's 1934 Novella GOODBYE, MR. CHIPS, ... 61

Session #16 of The Teacher and Student in Literature on Saying "Goodbye" to GOODBYE, MR. CHIPS 64

Bonus Session of The Teacher and Student in Literature on the 1934 British (But Universal?) Mr. Chips and His 1962 American Television "Twilight Zone" Version 67

Session #17 of The Teacher and Student in Literature on the Schoolmarm in Literature and on the 1955 Hollywood Movie "Good Morning, Miss Dove" 71

Bonus Session of the Teacher and Student in Literature on the Third-Grade Pupils in the "Miss Peach" Newspaper Comic Strip 77

Session #18 of The Teacher and Student in Literature on Brand-New Teacher Ursula Brangwen and Williams, Her Most Challenging Student, from D.H. Lawrence's 1915 Novel THE RAINBOW.. 79

Bonus Session of The Teacher and Student in Literature on Robert Coover's 2016 Short But Not Simple Story "The Hanging of the Schoolmarm".. 81

Bonus Session of The Teacher and Student in Literature on Teaching Some One Some Thing (or Something, Anything) Inspired by E. L. Konigsburg's 1966 Young Adult Novel THE VIEW FROM SATURDAY 85

Session #19 of The Teacher and Student in Literature on the 1937 Star-Studded Novel THE EDUCATION OF H*Y*M*A*N K*A*P*L*A*N 90

Session #20 of The Teacher and Student in Literature on the Classroom in Leo Rosten's THE EDUCATION OF H*Y*M*A*N K*A*P*L*A*N 94

Session #21 of The Teacher and Student in Literature on Muriel Spark's 1962 Novel THE PRIME OF MISS JEAN BRODIE 104

Session #22 of The Teacher and Student in Literature on Perspective and Politics in THE PRIME OF MISS JEAN BRODIE....... 108

Session #23 of The Teacher and Student in Literature on Morality and Ethics in THE PRIME OF MISS JEAN BRODIE 116

Bonus Session of The Teacher and Student in Literature on the Cult of Personality in School Fiction: Jean Brodie's "Set" of Impressionable Girls and the Boys of the "Dead Poets Society" 122

Bonus Session Project: An Oral Presentation on Remarkable Teachers and Students in Children's and Young Adult Literature....... 124

Session #24 of The Teacher and Student in Literature on Bel Kaufman's 1964 Novel UP THE DOWN STAIRCASE........................... 128

Session #25 of The Teacher and Student in Literature on the
"Hey, Teach" of UP THE DOWN STAIRCASE 132

Session #26 of The Teacher and Student in Literature on the
Style and the Students of UP THE DOWN STAIRCASE 135

Session #27 of The Teacher and Student in Literature on How
Hollywood Made Bel Kaufman's Unique School Novel Into a
Conventional Movie... 144

Session #28 of The Teacher and Student in Literature on the
Most Remarkable Fictional Teacher and Mentor of the Fall 2020
Course... 151

Kudos From Students in the Online Course of The Teacher and
Student in Literature.. 169

Author/Editor Robert Eidelberg's Books With A Built-In Teacher 171

About Educator/Author Robert Eidelberg... 173

WELCOME TO THE EMAIL CORRESPONDENCE COURSE BOOK FOR THE STUDY OF THE TEACHER AND STUDENT IN LITERATURE

First there was a special topics live on-campus English Department course – The Teacher and Student in Literature – created by me in 2015 for undergraduates at Hunter College of the City University of New York (many of the students majoring or minoring in English, some with the intention of becoming secondary school English teachers). But also with more than its fair share (however that's determined) of students majoring in sociology, psychology, and philosophy and taking the course out of sheer interest (it happens!) as well as for connections to the norms of those majors. Not to mention (but here goes) the course's heavy emphasis on creative writing as differentiated from academic writing (not so incidentally satisfying a graduation requirement for courses in "creative expression").

Then came the Pandemic of 2020 (an ironic year for a disease we should have "seen" coming) and an online version of The Teacher and Student in Literature with no room to be had on campus and no Zoom online. That course – 28 sessions online from August 2020 to December 2020 – is now (turn some pages) the course captured in this book.

You can *take* this "do-it-yourself" and "built-in-teacher" course as a student intrigued by the cultural nature and philosophy and practice of teaching (mostly in the United States and Great Britain) through reading and writing about remarkable (fictional but "for real") teachers (remarkably good and remarkably bad) and their challenging students or you can "take" the course as someone interested in perhaps going on to *teach* it on the high school or college level.

Like me back in the fall of 2020, you will not know what your colleagues (the students, the teacher) look like or aurally sound like but you will, via a correspondence course use of grammatical email, know what they think like, feel like, imagine like, and stylistically "sound" like. As you "take" or "teach" this email correspondence version of The Teacher and Student in Literature (The Teacher and Student in Email?), you will also come upon examples of academic writing and creative writing of students who originally wrote over the course of a semester for my eyes and ears (and those of their "course partners"). These students are now going public with their responses to my academic and creative writing prompts to their analytical abilities and their imaginative minds. A particular thank you to those who frequently let me know which prompts they found to be not only intriguing, challenging, and fun but also more than remotely worth their time and effort during trying times sheltered at home.

Robert Eidelberg

COLLEAGUE PROFILE / ENGLISH 25147 THE TEACHER AND STUDENT IN LITERATURE / MR. EIDELBERG / FALL 2020

(Note: This online course does NOT have a Zoom component)

_____ The first name you want to be known as (and called on as) in this class

_____ Your legal first name

_____ Your legal last name

Your gender pronoun preference (she, he, they): _____

_____ Your most reliable email contact number (the one you check regularly)

_____ Your best, and usually picked up, telephone or cellphone number

Your complete home address, including apartment number, borough, zip code

_____

The city _____, the state _____, and the country _____ you were born in – and the year _____ that you came to the United States if you weren't born in the United States

Your student level at Hunter College (circle just one): upper freshman / lower sophomore / upper sophomore / lower junior / upper junior / senior / graduating senior / senior citizen auditor

Current or likely major: _____

Current or likely minor: _____

Current or likely career or profession, and/or current fulltime job:
_____

The name, type (public, charter, private, parochial, boarding) and geographic location of the high school you attended and the year you graduated:

Name _____
Type of high school _____
Location _____
Graduation year: _____

Think back on a high school you attended and on the teachers and students in it. If one of these individuals were to commit the crime of murder against another one of these individuals (as actually happens in a fairly recent mystery novel set in an American high school), who would be killed, who would the killer be, what was the killer's motive, and exactly where and how in the school did the murder take place? Tell us all of that – right now – in the limited space below (continue on the back if absolutely necessary).

Should you be curious as to how one Hunter College student made use of that ridiculously "limited space" at the bottom of this course's Colleague Profile, here is **Rifath Islam's creative take** on a secondary school scene of the crime. It's a killer of a story.

Mister Dargahi, resident chemistry teacher at Manhattan Center High School, was mostly known for his eerily calm demeanor. Though many saw him as one of the more highly educated teachers in the school, they often avoided his presence altogether due to his random bursts of ill-tempered rage and his unappreciated sarcastic humor. Dargahi was known to be one of the best teachers in the school, constantly receiving the highest rating year after year, and though many of his students often came out of his class stressed, almost none of them received anything lower than an 80 come the end of the term. On the contrary, maybe most of his students were too scared to fail, as it was not uncommon for Dargahi to off-handedly make jokes about being the next candidate for Breaking Bad, listing off his extensive knowledge of deadly chemicals without a second thought.

However, this was not the case for 15-year-old sophomore Matthew Espinal who, no matter what he did, could not seem to focus in class. If it were just a matter of failing grades, that would be one thing, but Dargahi seemed to always find himself holding back his rage when Matthew would leave the class every day after mouthing off and disrupting the whole class. Dargahi found himself at his wit's end near the end of the semester; he knew that if the kid stayed in the his class that his rating would drop drastically, but Dargahi couldn't seem to find any other solution to his problem.

Until he came up with an entirely new lesson plan involving the chemical breakdown of drinking water. Come Matthew's lab period, Dargahi just "accidentally" put slightly too much mercury in the student's water sample. Initially, the sample was meant to only put Matthew in the hospital for the rest of the semester, making him miss the end-of-year exam that would determine Dargahi's teacher rating, but when the boy was pronounced dead on the way to the hospital, well, at least Dargahi got what he wanted.

INTRODUCTORY SESSION #1 OF THE TEACHER AND STUDENT IN LITERATURE, AND THE WALT WHITMAN POEM "WHEN I HEARD THE LEARN'D ASTRONOMER"

Hunter College of the City University of New York
Department of English Special Topics Course 25147
The Teacher and Student in Literature

Instructor: Mr. Robert Eidelberg / Semester: Fall 2020
Instructor's Office Hours: By appointment at course email: glamor62945@ mypacks.net
Class Meetings: Tuesdays and Thursdays evenings starting promptly at 5:35 and ending at 6:50
Room: 413 in Hunter West

Course Description, Syllabus, and Learning Objectives for English 25147: The Teacher and Student in Literature

School's in – and fictional teachers are for real. Meet and get to personally and professionally know a select class of them as they speak for themselves from novels, novellas, short stories, stage plays, poems, essays, popular movies, and comic strips. And, from the other side of the teacher's desk, hear from their students – a diverse group who are not afraid to answer back.

In this course you will become schooled in both teacher lit and in the philosophy, sociology, and politics of schooling in the United States and Western Europe – the societal norms and values and the cultural history that fictional teachers not only reflect, represent, and reinforce but also can challenge, rebel against, and subvert. English 25147 is a substantial reading course, critical thinking course, creative writing course, and talking-regularly-in-class course. There are no exams, quizzes, and papers as such, but there is a variety of front-of-the-room individual and group oral presentations and, at home, a range of imaginative written projects and activities.

Okay, class, scribble down (yes, scribble) some quick first-impression notes to yourself on any of the ways that a 2016 New Yorker magazine cartoon by artist B. Smaller can be understood to function as the "anti-syllabus" to this course as just described.

This single-panel cartoon is set in a suburban kitchen soon after breakfast (still visible in the scene's background on a kitchen table are a container of milk, a box of dry cereal, and one apparently empty cereal bowl with a spoon resting in it). In the foreground is a small boy (second- or third-grader?) who is declining the outerwear and packed school lunchbox his mother is about to hand to him. Instead, the boy says to his mother (and the caption to the cartoon states): "I've decided to work from home today."

In this correspondence course on THE TEACHER AND STUDENT IN LITERATURE, the words you will be reading will come from the following texts and literary works that you will need to own, rent, or borrow:

The Literature That Needs to Be Gotten at the Very Start of the Term

So You Think You Might Like to Teach:
23 Fictional Teachers (for Real!) Model
How to Become and Remain a Successful Teacher
by Robert Eidelberg (short work of mostly American fiction and non-fiction)
Penguin/Xlibris edition, 2013, ISBN 9781479798148

Staying After School: 19 Students (for Real!) Have the Next Best What-if Word on Remarkable Fictional Teachers and Their Often Challenging Classes
by Robert Eidelberg (with 19 Hunter College undergraduate students in the English Department special topics course "The Teacher and Student in Literature," 2016 - 2017 academic year)
Penguin/Xlibris edition, 2017, ISBN 9781543448009

The Blackboard Jungle by Evan Hunter (1954 American novel)
(any edition, softcover or hardcover)

Teacher Man by Frank McCourt (2005 American memoir)
(any edition, softcover or hardcover)

The Literature That Needs to Be Gotten a Bit Later Into the Term

Goodbye, Mr. Chips by James Hilton (1934 British novella)
Acra Foundation reprint edition, 2013, ISBN 9781492877462
(or any other inexpensive new or used edition)

*The Education of H*Y*M*A*N K*A*P*L*A*N* by Leo Rosten
(1937 short American novel published under the penname Leonard Q. Ross)
Harcourt reprint edition, 1965, ISBN 9780156278119

The Prime of Miss Jean Brodie by Muriel Spark (1962 short British novel)
HarperPerennial P.S. reprint edition, 2009, ISBN 9780061711299

Up the Down Staircase by Bel Kaufman (American novel, 1964)
(any softcover or hardcover edition)

AND THE WORDS YOU WILL FIND YOURSELF THINKING AND WRITING (both academically and creatively) will be "prompted" by the course instructor, Mr. Eidelberg, then proofread out loud every time you think you're done with them (because the ear often catches what the eye fails to sees – such as missing words and syllables, awkward constructions, and ungrammatical expressions), and, only then, sent to Mr. Eidelberg at this course's email address and to your course partner at theirs.

SOME COMMENTS ABOUT AND REACTIONS TO FORMAL EDUCATION *to be responded to in writing (cogently, coherently, cohesively,) with those responses emailed only to Professor Eidelberg:*

1. **"I've decided to work from home today"** (the caption to the 2016 "New Yorker" magazine cartoon by artist B. Smaller that appears on the first page of this Introductory Session to the Course of Study and Syllabus:

Prompt:
In what ways might this cartoon be considered the "anti-syllabus" to our course?

2. **"Life seemed to be an educator's practical joke in which you spent the first half learning and the second half learning that ....."**

Prompt:
Complete the above statement by American humorist Russell Baker from his 1983 book BACK TO THE DUMP.

3. Walt Whitman's poem "When I Heard the Learn'd Astronomer" (with the word "learn'd" pronounced no differently from the one-syllable word "learned") appears below.

When I heard the learn'd astronomer,
When the proofs, the figures, were ranged in columns
before me,
When I was shown the charts and diagrams, to add, divide,
and measure them,
When I, sitting, heard the learn'd astronomer where he
lectured with much
applause in the lecture room,
How soon unaccountable I became tired and sick,
Till rising and gliding out I wandered off by myself,
In the mystical moist night air, and from time to time,
Looked up in perfect silence at the stars.

Prompt:
Describe, in cogent, coherent, and cohesive academic writing, what you think the speaker of the poem's attitude is toward formal education, and provide the key diction details of the poem that helped you to come to that conclusion. (Give this question careful thought and Whitman's poem at least a second or third reading; do not jump to a quick and easy conclusion.) After you have thought about and possibly talked with someone else about the poem (and please do not shortchange or short-circuit your ability to analyze on your own), consider how **Hunter College student Jessica Chu** took account of the "unaccountable."

The speaker's attitude toward formal education in Walt Whitman's poem "When I Heard the Learn'd Astronomer" seems to be a negative one. Attending a lecture by a renowned astronomer, the speaker is given the mathematical reasonings, the charts, the graphs, all the data to prove what the astronomer is trying to explain in his lecture. Overwhelmed, the speaker walks away, goes outside, and all of a sudden, he experiences the night air as "mystical" and the stars as being "in perfect silence" – all in contrast to the lecture room he has fled.

In eight lines, American poet Walt Whitman has painted a clear image of what anyone who has been present in a traditional classroom environment may have emotionally felt. Sometimes, classrooms are stale and cold; you are given all the tools you need to mathematically prove a function, but there is no mythical element; however, sometimes there are things that people need to experience and feel for themselves. A "learn'd" astronomer may himself find all his data fascinating, but an educator needs to convey why his subject is worth learning – he needs to provide an answer to the question "Why would students care about this?"

SESSION #2 OF THE TEACHER AND STUDENT IN LITERATURE ON REMARKABLE, ALBEIT FICTIONAL, TEACHERS

Review your scribbled thoughts from the Introductory Session on how B. Smaller's 2016 New Yorker magazine cartoon functions (both visually and verbally) as a kind of "anti-syllabus" to the course description provided you on The Teacher and Student in Literature. Do some additional thinking and scribbling as to how this is true first for a "live" on-campus version of the course and then how it is also true, *but differently true*, for a remote online version of the course.

AN AMAZING ASSORTMENT (from children's lit and young adult lit)
All of the following academic "prompts" are to be responded to in writing (cogently, coherently, cohesively) and those responses sent to Mr. Eidelberg at the course email.

Headmistress Miss Trunchbull, in Roald Dahl's 1988 young adult novel MATILDA, says to the quite young, inexperienced, and very sweet (and aptly named) teacher Miss Honey: "My idea of a perfect school is one that has no children in it at all."

Prompt: *Huh? What's with Headmistress Trunchbull (and her Dickensian name)? What attitude do you hear behind her words?*

The opening sentence to Richard Peck's 2004 young adult novel THE TEACHER'S FUNERAL states: "If your teacher has to die, August isn't a bad time of year for it."

Prompt: *How can that be true? And if it is, for whom is it true?*

A textual excerpt from a bit down the first page of HOORAY FOR DIFFENDOOFER DAY (a children's picture book set in Diffendoofer School in the fictional American town of Dinkerville; drawings and text were begun by the famous writer and illustrator Dr. Seuss in 1989 and completed after Dr. Seuss died by Jack Prelutsky and Lane Smith in 2015):

"Our school is at the corner / Of Dinkzoober and Dinkzott.

"It looks like any other school, / But we suspect it's not.

"I think we're learning lots of things / Not taught at other schools.

"Our teachers are remarkable, / They make up their own rules."

Prompt: *What's so "remarkable" about teachers who make up their own rules?*

OUR FIRST EXTENDED CREATIVE WRITING ASSIGNMENT (CW/HW)

A first draft of the following should be emailed to your newly assigned course partner before your polished version is emailed to Mr. Eidelberg; partners should write back to each other detailing specifically what it is they like about each other's letter (and why) and constructively making no more than one helpful suggestion for improvement (if needed).

Summon up a remarkable ("worthy of being or likely to be noticed or remembered") teacher from your past as a student and think long and hard about what exactly made her or him "remarkable" (in either positive or negative ways since teachers can be remarkably good and remarkably bad). Capture these personal and professional qualities, actions, moments, and quotable words in a well-written and detailed "Dear ..." letter to that actual teacher (even if she or he is not now alive or locatable – and regardless of whether you would actually mail it or email it off). Either after or before you write your own remarkable teacher letter, consider checking out a model example on pages 101 - 103 of Mr. Eidelberg's text STAYING AFTER SCHOOL.

SESSION #3 OF THE TEACHER AND STUDENT IN LITERATURE ON WHO'S THE TEACHER, WHO'S THE STUDENT, AND LEO TOLSTOY'S 1886 SHORT STORY "THE THREE HERMITS"

REMARKABLE TEACHER LETTERS

If you are in a position to, course partners should share their remarkable teacher letters with each other and jointly compile a list of qualities, characteristics, values, and behaviors that you will consult each time you meet a new fictional remarkable teacher in this course.

THE THREE HERMITS

(an 1886 short story by Leo Tolstoy; a public domain online version is reproduced below without any changes by Mr. Eidelberg to its use of British spelling or to the standard British use of double quotation marks within single quotations marks rather than the other way around, which is the American style)

Read before today's session this classic 19th-century short story by the Russian writer Leo Tolstoy – some have called it the best story about education ever written. Then, using my pack of prompts *below* (and, most importantly, any of *your own questions and concerns* about the story), "scribble" (I mean it!) legible notes (*to* yourself and *for* yourself) as you read Tolstoy's story. Finally, consult your "scribbled notes" in any email or phone discussion you have about this not-all-that-well-known Tolstoy story with a course partner or another interested person.

A Pack of Prompts for the short story "The Three Hermits"

Prompt #1: How is this Russian short story at all about teaching and learning? Be specific and detailed.

Prompt #2: What questions, concerns, and confusions that you have do you want pursued in any discussion of the story?

Prompt #3: What possible relevance does the story have to our lives in the twenty-first century?

AN OLD LEGEND CURRENT IN THE VOLGA DISTRICT

'And in praying use not vain repetitions, as the Gentiles do: for they think that they shall be heard for their much speaking. Be not therefore like unto them: for your Father knoweth what things ye have need of, before ye ask Him.' – Matt. vi. 7, 8.

A BISHOP was sailing from Archangel to the Solovtsk Monastery; and on the same vessel were a number of pilgrims on their way to visit the shrines at that place. The voyage was a smooth one. The wind favourable, and the weather fair. The pilgrims lay on deck, eating, or sat in groups talking to one another. The Bishop, too, came on deck, and as he was pacing up and down, he noticed a group of men standing near the prow and listening to a fisherman who was pointing to the sea and telling them something. The Bishop stopped, and looked in the direction in which the man was pointing. He could see nothing, however, but the sea glistening in the sunshine. He drew nearer to listen, but when the man saw him, he took off his cap and was silent. The rest of the people also took off their caps, and bowed.

'Do not let me disturb you, friends,' said the Bishop. 'I came to hear what this good man was saying.'

'The fisherman was telling us about the hermits,' replied one, a tradesman, rather bolder than the rest.

'What hermits?' asked the Bishop, going to the side of the vessel and seating himself on a box. 'Tell me about them. I should like to hear. What were you pointing at?'

'Why, that little island you can just see over there,' answered the man, pointing to a spot ahead and a little to the right. 'That is the island where the hermits live for the salvation of their souls.'

'Where is the island?' asked the Bishop. 'I see nothing.'

'There, in the distance, if you will please look along my hand. Do you see that little cloud? Below it and a bit to the left, there is just a faint streak. That is the island.'

The Bishop looked carefully, but his unaccustomed eyes could make out nothing but the water shimmering in the sun.

'I cannot see it,' he said. 'But who are the hermits that live there?'

'They are holy men,' answered the fisherman. 'I had long heard tell of them, but never chanced to see them myself till the year before last.'

And the fisherman related how once, when he was out fishing, he had been stranded at night upon that island, not knowing where he was. In the morning, as he wandered about the island, he came across an earth hut, and met an old man standing near it. Presently two others came out, and after having fed him, and dried his things, they helped him mend his boat.

'And what are they like?' asked the Bishop.

'One is a small man and his back is bent. He wears a priest's cassock and is very old; he must be more than a hundred, I should say. He is so old that the white of his beard is taking a greenish tinge, but he is always smiling, and his face is as bright as an angel's from heaven. The second is taller, but he also is very old. He wears tattered, peasant coat. His beard is broad, and of a yellowish grey colour. He is a strong man. Before I had time to help him, he turned my boat over as if it were only a pail. He, too, is kindly and cheerful. The third is tall, and has a beard as white as snow and reaching to his knees. He is stern, with over-hanging eyebrows; and he wears nothing but a mat tied round his waist.'

'And did they speak to you?' asked the Bishop.

'For the most part they did everything in silence and spoke but little even to one another. One of them would just give a glance, and the others would understand him. I asked the tallest whether they had lived there long. He frowned, and muttered something as if he were angry; but the oldest one took his hand and smiled, and then the tall one was quiet. The oldest one only said: "Have mercy upon us," and smiled.'

While the fisherman was talking, the ship had drawn nearer to the island.

'There, now you can see it plainly, if your Grace will please to look,' said the tradesman, pointing with his hand.

The Bishop looked, and now he really saw a dark streak – which was the island. Having looked at it a while, he left the prow of the vessel, and going to the stern, asked the helmsman:

'What island is that?'

'That one,' replied the man, 'has no name. There are many such in this sea.'

'Is it true that there are hermits who live there for the salvation of their souls?'

'So it is said, your Grace, but I don't know if it's true. Fishermen say they have seen them; but of course they may only be spinning yarns.'

'I should like to land on the island and see these men,' said the Bishop. 'How could I manage it?'

'The ship cannot get close to the island,' replied the helmsman, 'but you might be rowed there in a boat. You had better speak to the captain.'

The captain was sent for and came.

'I should like to see these hermits,' said the Bishop. 'Could I not be rowed ashore?'

The captain tried to dissuade him.

'Of course it could be done,' said he, 'but we should lose much time. And if I might venture to say so to your Grace, the old men are not worth your pains. I have heard say that they are foolish old fellows, who understand nothing, and never speak a word, any more than the fish in the sea.'

'I wish to see them,' said the Bishop, 'and I will pay you for your trouble and loss of time. Please let me have a boat.'

There was no help for it; so the order was given. The sailors trimmed the sails, the steersman put up the helm, and the ship's course was set for the island. A chair was placed at the prow for the Bishop, and he sat there, looking ahead. The passengers all collected at the prow, and gazed at the island. Those who had the sharpest eyes could presently make out the rocks on it, and then a mud hut was seen. At last one man saw the hermits themselves. The captain brought a telescope and, after looking through it, handed it to the Bishop.

'It's right enough. There are three men standing on the shore. There, a little to the right of that big rock.'

The Bishop took the telescope, got it into position, and he saw the three men: a tall one, a shorter one, and one very small and bent, standing on the shore and holding each other by the hand.

The captain turned to the Bishop.

'The vessel can get no nearer in than this, your Grace. If you wish to go ashore, we must ask you to go in the boat, while we anchor here.'

The cable was quickly let out, the anchor cast, and the sails furled. There was a jerk, and the vessel shook. Then a boat having been lowered, the oarsmen jumped in, and the Bishop descended the ladder and took his seat. The men pulled at their oars, and the boat moved rapidly towards the island. When they came within a stone's throw they saw three old men: a tall one with only a mat tied round his waist: a shorter one in a tattered peasant coat, and a very old one bent with age and wearing an old cassock – all three standing hand in hand.

The oarsmen pulled in to the shore, and held on with the boathook while the Bishop got out.

The old men bowed to him, and he gave them his benediction, at which they bowed still lower. Then the Bishop began to speak to them.

'I have heard,' he said, 'that you, godly men, live here saving your own souls, and praying to our Lord Christ for your fellow men. I, an unworthy servant of Christ, am called, by God's mercy, to keep and teach His flock. I wished to see you, servants of God, and to do what I can to teach you, also.'

The old men looked at each other smiling, but remained silent.

'Tell me,' said the Bishop, 'what you are doing to save your souls, and how you serve God on this island.'

The second hermit sighed, and looked at the oldest, the very ancient one. The latter smiled, and said:

'We do not know how to serve God. We only serve and support ourselves, servant of God.'

'But how do you pray to God?' asked the Bishop.

'We pray in this way,' replied the hermit. 'Three are ye, three are we, have mercy upon us.'

And when the old man said this, all three raised their eyes to heaven, and repeated:

'Three are ye, three are we, have mercy upon us!'

The Bishop smiled.

'You have evidently heard something about the Holy Trinity,' said he. 'But you do not pray aright. You have won my affection, godly men. I see you wish to please the Lord, but you do not know how to serve Him. That is not the way to pray; but listen to me, and I will teach you. I will teach you, not a way of my own, but the way in which God in the Holy Scriptures has commanded all men to pray to Him.'

And the Bishop began explaining to the hermits how God had revealed Himself to men; telling them of God the Father, and God the Son, and God the Holy Ghost.

'God the Son came down on earth,' said he, 'to save men, and this is how He taught us all to pray. Listen and repeat after me: "Our Father."'

And the first old man repeated after him, 'Our Father,' and the second said, 'Our Father,' and the third said, 'Our Father.'

'Which art in heaven,' continued the Bishop.

The first hermit repeated, 'Which art in heaven,' but the second blundered over the words, and the tall hermit could not say them properly. His hair had grown over his mouth so that he could not speak plainly. The very old hermit, having no teeth, also mumbled indistinctly.

The Bishop repeated the words again, and the old men repeated them after him. The Bishop sat down on a stone, and the old men stood before him, watching his mouth, and repeating the words as he uttered them. And all day long the Bishop laboured, saying a word twenty, thirty, a hundred times over, and the old men repeated it after him. They blundered, and he corrected them, and made them begin again.

The Bishop did not leave off till he had taught them the whole of the Lord's prayer so that they could not only repeat it after him, but could say it by themselves. The middle one was the first to know it, and to repeat the whole of it alone. The Bishop made him say it again and again, and at last the others could say it too.

It was getting dark, and the moon was appearing over the water, before the Bishop rose to return to the vessel. When he took leave of the old men, they all bowed down to the ground before him. He raised them, and kissed each of them, telling them to pray as he had taught them. Then he got into the boat and returned to the ship.

And as he sat in the boat and was rowed to the ship he could hear the three voices of the hermits loudly repeating the Lord's prayer. As the boat drew near the vessel their voices could no longer be heard, but they could still be seen in the moonlight, standing as he had left them on the shore, the shortest in the middle, the tallest on the right, the middle one on the left. As soon as the Bishop had reached the vessel and got on board, the anchor was weighed and the sails unfurled. The wind filled them, and the ship sailed away, and the Bishop took a seat in the stern and watched the island they had left. For a time he could still see the hermits, but presently they disappeared from sight, though the island was still visible. At last it too vanished, and only the sea was to be seen, rippling in the moonlight.

The pilgrims lay down to sleep, and all was quiet on deck. The Bishop did not wish to sleep, but sat alone at the stern, gazing at the sea where the island was no longer visible, and thinking of the good old men. He thought how pleased they had been to learn the Lord's prayer; and he thanked God for having sent him to teach and help such godly men.

So the Bishop sat, thinking, and gazing at the sea where the island had disappeared. And the moonlight flickered before his eyes, sparkling, now here, now there, upon the waves. Suddenly he saw something white and shining, on the bright path which the moon cast across the sea. Was it a seagull, or the little gleaming sail of some small boat? The Bishop fixed his eyes on it, wondering.

'It must be a boat sailing after us,' thought he 'but it is overtaking us very rapidly. It was far, far away a minute ago, but now it is much nearer. It cannot be a boat, for I can see no sail; but whatever it may be, it is following us, and catching us up.'

And he could not make out what it was. Not a boat, nor a bird, nor a fish! It was too large for a man, and besides a man could not be out there in the midst of the sea. The Bishop rose, and said to the helmsman:

'Look there, what is that, my friend? What is it?' the Bishop repeated, though he could now see plainly what it was – the three hermits running upon the water, all gleaming white, their grey beards shining, and approaching the ship as quickly as though it were not morning.

The steersman looked and let go the helm in terror.

'Oh Lord! The hermits are running after us on the water as though it were dry land!'

The passengers hearing him, jumped up, and crowded to the stern. They saw the hermits coming along hand in hand, and the two outer ones beckoning the ship to stop. All three were gliding along upon the water without moving their feet. Before the ship could be stopped, the hermits had reached it, and raising their heads, all three as with one voice, began to say:

'We have forgotten your teaching, servant of God. As long as we kept repeating it we remembered, but when we stopped saying it for a time, a word dropped out, and now it has all gone to pieces. We can remember nothing of it. Teach us again.'

The Bishop crossed himself, and leaning over the ship's side, said:

'Your own prayer will reach the Lord, men of God. It is not for me to teach you. Pray for us sinners.'

And the Bishop bowed low before the old men; and they turned and went back across the sea. And a light shone until daybreak on the spot where they were lost to sight.

* * * * *

After you have thought about and possibly talked with someone else about this pack of prompts, you might want to consider how **Hunter College student Hudaiba Khatri** *put her thoughts on these prompts into analytical writing.*

Leo Tolstoy's short story "The Three Hermits" is about teaching and learning through the Bishop's guidance given to the hermits on how to pray correctly. The learning aspect is the hermits' reciting over and over again the Bishop's prayer to ensure that they learn it correctly and so can praise God correctly. When the Bishop is reciting the prayer for the hermits to memorize, he is the teacher. He stays there for hours helping the old hermits to memorize it correctly. He clearly says, "But you do not pray right," and works to correct it.

However, towards the end of the story when the hermits run after the Bishop, after they realize they have forgotten the prayer, in a way the hermits are the teachers: they taught the Bishop from their actions and through their kindness, instead of through a rigorous curriculum or rote memorization. The willingness of the hermits to correct themselves unhesitatingly during their education under the Bishop is admirable in comparison with the Bishop's subtle ego and arrogance. When the Bishop says at the end of the story that "It is not for me to teach you; pray for us sinners," it is clear that he has learned his lesson and now understands that prayer is something that is subjective to each person.

The part in the story where the hermits are almost walking on water was a bit confusing to me. I am assuming it was a religious reference to Christianity, but I didn't quite understand it. I think it might be a way to show the status given to the hermits' humility, since they can walk on water, and this might be a way for the Bishop to visually see the glory and peace the hermits possess.

In the United States in the 21st century, there is a strong emphasis on not only supporting what you believe but supporting it in an extremist way, allowing absolutely no room for discussion. This is similar to the mindset that the Bishop entered the hermits' island with: he was very clearly focused on teaching through a strict method and exact words. However, the lesson that we learn as readers of this story is through the Bishop's final acknowledgment of his arrogance.

Only when he realizes the error of his thinking is the Bishop able to appreciate the humility and individuality of the hermits. So I would say that the key lesson to be taken from Tolstoy's story is that we as individuals in a society need to listen before we speak and to truly try to understand another's perspective.

Prompt:
*Where in the following **1913 poem called "The Three Hermits" by the Irish poet William Butler Yeats** does it sound to you that Yeats was familiar with Tolstoy's 1886 short story of the same name and might have been affected and influenced by his reading of it?*

Three old hermits took the air
By a cold and desolate sea,
First was muttering a prayer,
Second rummaged for a flea;
On a windy stone, the third,
Giddy with his hundredth year,
Sang unnoticed like a bird:
"Though the Door of Death is near
And what waits behind the door,
Three times in a single day
I, though upright on the shore,
Fall asleep when I should pray."
So the first, but now the second:
"We're but given what we have earned,

When all thoughts and deeds are reckoned,
So it's plain to be discerned
That the shades of holy men
Who have failed, being weak of will,
Pass the Door of Birth again,
And are plagued by crowds, until
They've the passion to escape."
Moaned the other, "They are thrown
Into some most fearful shape."
But the second mocked his moan:
"They are not changed to anything,
Having loved God once, but maybe
To a poet or a king
Or a witty lovely lady."
While he'd rummaged rags and hair,
Caught and cracked his flea, the third,
Giddy with his hundredth year,
Sang unnoticed like a bird.

SESSION #4 OF THE TEACHER AND STUDENT IN LITERATURE ON "HELP WANTED, NEW TEACHER NEEDED," AND MISS READ'S 1955 NOVEL VILLAGE SCHOOL

SO YOU THINK YOU MIGHT LIKE TO TEACH

Read all of Chapter 1 in Mr. Eidelberg's text SO YOU THINK YOU MIGHT LIKE TO TEACH. The chapter is mostly about the American novel THEOPHILUS NORTH by Thornton Wilder and the title character's nine "ambitions" (career choices). Respond to the following prompts by email to Mr. Eidelberg.

Prompt #1: Based on all nine of North's "ambitions," would you say that he might have made a "remarkably good" or "remarkably bad" public school (not private school or parochial school) teacher – and why do you think that?

Prompt #2: What personality and character aspects did all (or most) of North's "ambitions" have in common that would work for or against his possible future success or failure on either the elementary or secondary school levels of the teaching profession?

*After you have given some thought to the above two prompts but before you email your academic writing to Mr. Eidelberg, compare your ideas with those of **Hunter College students Shelly Uzagir and Danny Liang** and revise your initial responses as you see fit.*

From Shelly Uzagir:

Based on all nine of Theophilus North's nine "ambitions," I would say that he might have made a remarkably bad public school teacher. Although it is arguable that North might have made a wonderful teacher based on his interest in archeology, anthropology, and even his fascination with becoming a missionary to "primitive" people. North would have an abundance of knowledge and experience to share with his students, not to mention his fifth and sixth ambitions (actor and magician) would have equipped him with a an incredible teaching tool, the ability to captivate an audience, in this case, his students.

However, I say he might have made a remarkably bad public school teacher because of his inability to be selfless and truthful. Everyone says that teaching is a noble profession; I would say it's also an altruistic career. Selfless teaching is having an evolving lesson plan. It's being aware that students are at different levels and you must modify your teaching to ensure the entire classroom is learning – not just the students who are "easy" to teach. Catering to students in that way takes patience, understanding, and selflessness. It's also important to be a truthful teacher, especially since most public schools have an academic honor code based on trust and honesty.

In addition, North wanted to be a "free man" with no boss over him. Teachers influence the quality of education that students receive and are key aspects to students' overall academic learning, but teachers are not believed to have too much control over the curriculum and are mandated to follow a model. Therefore, North would not be a "free man" working as a teacher in a public school system.

From Danny Jiang:

Theophilus North becomes a teacher not out of immediate desire, but of necessity. According to Mr. Eidelberg's text STAYING AFTER SCHOOL, North "backs" into teaching as 'a safety net.'" This follows a list of ambitions North has held throughout his life, which include the following: saint, anthropologist, archaeologist, detective, actor, magician, lover, rascal, free man. Considering all of these ambitions that North once pursued, I would argue that he would make a "remarkably good" public school teacher. North's first ambition, to be a saint, relates to Richard Dadier's experience in the novel THE BLACKBOARD JUNGLE looking at the classroom he will soon teach in, for Dadier "looked out over the rows of empty seats, feeling something like a priest in a new parish awaiting his Sunday congregation." To teach is to also "preach" your learnings: what you have learned in life, and what you have learned about your subject.

The ambition of becoming an anthropologist is a result of North's secularization of his ambition to become a saint, which he defines as being a "missionary among primitive people." This ambition relates to the traits of a remarkably good teacher, one who devotes their life to the betterment of those who at the time may know less. Next, North turns his attention toward becoming an archaeologist and a detective, both of which uncover truths to share with others – just as a teacher would in and out of class. His next ambitions are to be an amazing actor and magician. These ambitions present themselves as dreams that may not mesh well with teaching, but in fact, do so very well. To be a lover in the context of teaching means that North would have to put aside his own differences for the sake of his students – love, in this case, realizes the "selflessness, truthfulness, and celibacy" which North thought he was incapable of when pursuing his first ambition of becoming a saint. His wish to become a rascal further reinforces this: in his definition of rascal as someone who always lives by their wits, he is challenging himself to always be ahead of whatever is thrown at him – disobedient students, poor administration, deadlines and more - and remain a steadfast "lover" to his career and students.

Finally, North reaches his last ambition, which is to be a free man. He tells himself that he wants to be "not caged and incarcerated" and that his lack of desire to enter the fields of banking, law, and politics is the result of the fact that he wants "no boss over [him], or only the lightest of supervisions." He even stops working as a full-time teacher to work as a part-time tutor, to reinforce this desire to be a free man. Though this may deem him as not a "remarkably good" teacher (for what great teacher would quit their job?), I would still argue that all of his nine ambitions have made him "remarkably good." To be a (good) teacher, after all, is to remain a student for one's whole life. North embodies this by learning what he wants out of each of the ambitions he has had and channels them into his decision about leaving a full-time teaching post, and taking up a part-time tutoring gig. In leaving his job, North teaches himself that his wish to be a free man is realized by his time as a teacher and funnily enough, he still chooses to teach, though not as a public teacher but a tutor.

STAYING AFTER SCHOOL

Read all of Chapter 3 in Mr. Eidelberg's text STAYING AFTER SCHOOL. The chapter is about the hiring of a new elementary school teacher in Great Britain and comes from a chapter called "The New Teacher" in the 1955 novel VILLAGE SCHOOL by "Miss Read" (penname of Dora Saint). Although the chapter never actually produces the actual teacher-wanted "advert" (British short form for "advertisement" comparable to, but longer than, our American "ad"), you should be able to mentally make up a list of the job "specs" (short for "specifications") from a close reading of and critical thinking about "The New Teacher" (note: don't miss the religious "requirements" for a teaching position in this non-parochial school).

Next, think about how many and which of those "specs" and personality and character qualities would apply, let's say, to possible new hires if you were the President of Hunter College and looking to fill a teaching opening or vacancy in one of the college's departments (such as English, sociology, psychology, computer science, history, biology, music, art, political science, or whatever you choose). Finally, select ONE of the following creative writing activities and email your out loud proofread written result to both Mr. Eidelberg and your partner.

CW/HW Choice "A": Create an actual ad (that has the look and sound of an ad) that could be published nationwide to attract the best job applicants to this particular teaching position at Hunter College; or

CW/HW Choice "B": Create a job interview (using dialogue) between a fictional version of the President of Hunter College who wants what is best for Hunter's students and an eager applicant who desperately wants (and not just because the pay is so good) to teach on the college level, preferably in a public college, and ideally at Hunter College of the City University of New York.

Here is how Hunter College student Anika Bradley handled CW/HW Choice "B":

Excerpts from a fictional job interview:
Hunter College Sociology

Hunter College President: You just completed your doctoral degree this year, correct?

Applicant: Yes, that's correct.

HC President: So aside from your work in graduate school for your master's and doctoral degrees, you have no prior teaching experience?

Eager Applicant: While yes that's true, my ethnographic research for my urban sociology PhD has provided me with extensive experience studying metropolitan school systems through sitting in on lessons and assisting in classrooms from elementary school through graduate programs. My sociological background is also a key reason I would love to be a part of the City University of New York system rather than a private university.

HC President: During your studies what made you decide to go into the teaching profession rather than putting your degree towards another aspect of your field?

Eager Applicant: My love of what I do in the sociology field stems from a strong desire to understand the complexities of human interaction and what shapes society into the way it is today and has been in the past. As we're well aware, there's a consistent pattern in societies to grow and change with the times, along with our minds and opinions. These changes almost always come from our youth and the only way to continue the pattern of positive changes is through education. There's no better way for me to make use of my extensive research into the human mind and its patterns than by assisting the next generation in evolving our society. Before college, I hardly had any knowledge about the field, but my first sociology professor my freshman hear truly unlocked the passion for it within me and I hope to be able to do that for my students as well.

HC President: Excellent. Ass you've said, your field is all about the ever-changing world, so are you continuing your education or fieldwork while you'll be teaching?

Eager Applicant: I fully intend to continue my research outside of my teaching career. As much as my students will be learning from me, I will be learning from them as well. Being in an inner-city college environment is essential to my outside work and provides me with more insight into my field than almost anything else. It will also be nearly impossible for my continued studies to interfere with my teaching because the two are so essential to one another.

HC President: Take me through what one meeting of your class would be like.

Eager Applicant: A class in this department is so unlike any other because sociology isn't a class that can be taught out of a textbook. By the time a book has been out for five years, it's already basically outdated. In my class, I plan to center the focus around discussions as much as possible. Each meeting of the class will be focus around a different aspect of urban sociology, whether that be the education system, economics, poverty and class, housing, or racial inequality, just to name a few. I would expect that students will come to class having read the assigned handouts, typically selected chapters of varying ethnographies or theories. I don't want to waste class time having to read straight out of a book to catch people up, unless it's truly necessary to alleviate confusion. I want to start every class session by getting all the comments and questions out in the open from students, which usually leads fairly seamlessly into a discussion about the issues at hand.

HC President: How would you engage non-major students taking the introductory class who may not be as dedicated to the subject?

Eager Applicant: My philosophy of engaging the non-major students is to relate the studies directly back to their worldly experiences. Students going to Hunter College or any City University of New York school, really, are mostly coming from city backgrounds and are familiar with at least one or more issues in their city. Especially in the introductory courses, there's so much room to cater the class to specific issues the students want to focus on or feel drawn towards. By igniting that passion for certain issues within them, students feel that deeper connection to the study and its relevance in their lives.

Course Literature Reading Alert: you absolutely must have a copy (any edition) of the novel THE BLACKBOARD JUNGLE by Evan Hunter at hand because the next several sessions of the course are devoted to it.

SESSION #5 OF THE TEACHER AND STUDENT IN LITERATURE: "COVERING" EVAN HUNTER'S 1954 NOVEL THE BLACKBOARD JUNGLE

Find on YouTube for Evan Hunter's novel THE BLACKBOARD JUNGLE as many different front overs of Evan Hunter's novel as you can. Only one of them will be from a hardcover edition since THE BLACKBOARD JUNGLE was originally and unconventionally published in 1954 as a small paperback or "pocketbook" (costing 25 cents!) that could literally fit in a pants' pocket.

Print out all the various editions' covers and arrange them in date of publication order right up to the most recent 2017 softcover trade edition (which can't fit in a pants' pocket). Include, if you can, the cover art work of the DVD of the film version of the novel (called BLACKBOARD JUNGLE, without the THE).

A Pack of Prompts

Prompt #1:
Look at, analyze, and make some inferences about these covers and scribble down some notes on each of the several covers as to how they differ over time from one another and your thoughts as to why that might be. Speculate on possible publishing or cultural reasons from 1954 to 2017 for the specific visual changes you see in content, arrangement, composition, focus, perspective, and color as well as the verbal changes and diction choices you find in this "jungle" of covers representing more than six decades of continual re-publication and continuous printing.

Prompt #2:
As you can see, the front cover of the 1954 *paperback original* depicted a youngish white male high school teacher (wearing a suit and a bow tie), one noticeably buxom white adolescent female student, one black adolescent male student, and one white adolescent male student; squeezed between all this cover art and the title THE BLACKBOARD JUNGLE the following words appeared in small italics: *"A novel of juvenile delinquents."*

Of all the persons depicted on the 1954 cover, which one, if you had to pick one (and I'm saying that you do!), would you describe as the most "delinquent"? Give at least two reasons for your choice.

THE BLACKBOARD JUNGLE

Begin your reading of this first of our course's several novels on remarkable fictional teachers and their challenging students; email your "pack of prompt" responses to both Mr. Eidelberg and your course partner.

A Pack of Prompts

Prompt #1:
Read for this session at least the opening chapter of this three-part novel set in urban New York in the 1950's. It is always interesting and often instructive to take note of the opening sentences (or the first paragraph) of a work of fiction. What do you notice of interest about how author Evan Hunter (a penname) begins his first novel ever for the general reading public (Hunter had previously written, under the pseudonym "Ed McBain," a good many crime novels) – and what do you make of that opening paragraph?

Prompt #2:
Which particular characters that you might have expected to meet early on in this kind of novel don't we meet right away – and why might you, as the author, have intentionally structured the opening of this particular novel of yours in this way?

Prompt #3:
Who is the first "character" the author introduces his readers to, and how is this a potential major character? Speculate as to why Evan Hunter made that "author"-ial decision.

SESSION #6 OF THE TEACHER AND STUDENT IN LITERATURE ON PART ONE OF THE BLACKBOARD JUNGLE

THE BLACKBOARD JUNGLE by Evan Hunter / Part One

Read all of Part One; email your prompt responses to both Mr. Eidelberg and your course partner.

Prompt #1:
Whether you think first impressions of people matter or not, what are your first impressions of the various major and minor characters we are introduced to by the end of Part One? (Interestingly, "first impressions" is the subject of the opening lesson that fictional teacher Sylvia Barrett plans for the very first class of her teaching career in the work of literature – the novel UP THE DOWN STAIRCASE – that bookends our study of The Teacher and Student in Literature.)

Prompt #2:
Ponder the relative truth – so far in your reading – of the 1954 claim on the front cover of THE BLACKBOARD JUNGLE that it is "a novel of juvenile delinquents." Ponder, also, the relative truth of the loud (actually, shouted) declaration in the movie trailer (coming attraction) of the 1955 Hollywood feature film version of the novel that urban American adolescents are "terrorizing" the public school system in the United States.

SO YOU THINK YOU MIGHT LIKE TO TEACH

Read: pages 39 – 48 (top) of Chapter 3 for a foundation on the psychological mind games that students and teachers play

Read: pages 71 – 77 (top) of Chapter 5, which includes games teachers play with one another

Prompt:
If you think of a job interview (for any job) as a kind of psychological mind game played by the interviewer and the interviewee, which tactical game "moves" made by English Chair Stanley and by prospective teacher Rick Dadier impress you the most for game-playing – and why? Email your prompt response to both Mr. Eidelberg and your course partner.

Creative Writing Assignment (CW/HW)

"Remembering" a class discussion that we somehow never actually had (not even remotely!), as readers of other people's writing we can be purposefully and particularly helpful in our feedback if we make just these two comments in the margins of their written pieces: "well seen" and "well said." So, let's do that for writer Evan Hunter as good readers of Part One of his novel THE BLACKBOARD JUNGLE. Choose either a sentence, or a paragraph, or a short scene from anywhere in the first seven chapters of THE BLACKBOARD JUNGLE and write a fan letter to its author on what was so "well seen" or so "well said" (or both!) in that sentence, paragraph, or short scene of his. Choose well and wisely, honestly and personally – as both a reader of well-written novels and as a student who is learning how to write well yourself. Email your CW/HW to both Mr. Eidelberg and your course partner.

SESSION #7 OF THE TEACHER AND STUDENT IN LITERATURE ON PART TWO OF THE BLACKBOARD JUNGLE

THE BLACKBOARD JUNGLE by Evan Hunter / Part Two

Reading and Critical Thinking Prompts for All of Part Two of THE BLACKBOARD JUNGLE. Consider all five prompts and then respond in writing to three of them to both Mr. Eidelberg and your course partner.

1. What function do each of the following adult male characters play in author Evan Hunter's construction of the plot line of the story he is telling and the themes of his novel: the prospective teacher interviewed for the English vacancy just before Rick, the school's English Chair (who conducted the interviews and basically gave Rick the job), Principal Small (note the name), Josh, Mr. Manners, veteran teachers Lou Savoldi and Solly Klein?

2. What function do each of the following adolescent male characters play in author Evan Hunter's construction of the plot line of the story he is telling and the themes of his novel: Sullivan, Arthur Francis West, Morales, the other students in Rick's homeroom and in his English class?

3. Is Rick prejudiced against Black people? Who in the novel believes he is, and why? Who in the novel believes he isn't, and why? As someone reading this novel for the first time in a country currently politically divided on the issues of systemic racism, Black Lives Matter, white privilege, social and economic injustice, a call for rethinking of

how local police departments are funded, and a former president originally from New York City who campaigned in 2016 on "carnage" in American cities and who declared in 2020 that he will send "the military" to American cities experiencing "out-of-control" violence, how do you feel about the answer to the question "In the New York City of 1954, is public school teacher Rick Dadier (with immigrant ancestry) a prejudiced American citizen?"

4. Before starting on the writing of THE BLACKBOARD JUNGLE, Evan Hunter was a very successful writer of crime novels under the pen name Ed McBain. What aspects of the crime novel do you detect, if any, in THE BLACKBOARD JUNGLE? (If you have read any American crime novels or seen any 1940's black and white Hollywood examples of film noir, you might want to additionally think about similarities you notice between how they depict American women in general and how the two female characters in THE BLACKBOARD JUNGLE – who never meet, by the way – are portrayed.)

5. Historically over the years American public school teachers have been mostly female (though American teachers were *originally exclusively male*). Think about how this fact of gender might have affected taxpayer support as well as other kinds of non-financial support for public education in the history of the United States. Also, how might this fact of gender difference affect even today the very nature of the teaching and learning process in the fifty separate states that make up this nation?

SESSION #8 OF THE TEACHER AND STUDENT IN LITERATURE ON PART THREE OF THE BLACKBOARD JUNGLE

Respond in writing to both Mr. Eidelberg and your course partner on two of the following four reading and critical thinking prompts on the novel and its 1955 film version.

1. Let's "cover" the several book covers that the novel THE BLACKBOARD JUNGLE has had since it was first published sixty-six years ago in 1954. I believe the last cover, so far, was the one on the softcover trade (non-pocket-book) edition published in 2017 – and that is the edition that most of you probably have. There is, of course, the special cover to grace the only hardcover edition of THE BLACKBOARD JUNGLE, and a really well-known cover that was especially created for the 50th anniversary of Hunter's novel in 2004; some of you may have these editions. (If you want to see what these and other covers looked like, you can readily find most of them on the internet.)

2. Okay, so after you have completed the novel, compare and contrast the original 1954 pocket-book cover with at least one other cover and then respond to the following prompt: the front cover of the 1954 edition depicts all of the following in a variety of colors: a youngish white male high school teacher (wearing a suit and a bow tie), next to him one noticeably buxom white adolescent female student, one Black adolescent male student in the background, and one white adolescent male student holding an open switchblade knife (check out what this kind of knife looks like and how it works if you are not completely familiar with it). Squeezed between all this 1950's cover art and the book's title THE BLACKBOARD JUNGLE, the following words appear in much smaller italic print: "A novel of juvenile delinquents."

Now, look at the front cover of your edition (or, if you prefer, one of the editions shown on the internet) and, in coherent and cohesive academic writing, tell why you think that one of these two covers is a more honest and accurate depiction of Hunter's somewhat long but extraordinarily successful novel (millions and millions sold, and still selling worldwide in something like two dozen different languages). If you were asked to design a new cover for a forthcoming edition of THE BLACKBOARD JUNGLE, which elements would you place on it in order to truly depict what you believe the novel is essentially about (and its relevance to readers today, including your colleagues in English 25147).

3. The Hollywood feature film version of THE BLACKBOARD JUNGLE was rushed into production and was released in 1955 (just a year later) because the novel was such a major hit with the American reading public. Directed by Richard Brooks (and available free on YouTube), it also caused a sensation (because it was sensational?). The trailer to the film (the preview of "coming attractions" shown in America's movie houses the week before the film opened nationally) had a narrator's voice declare (actually, SHOUT) that urban American adolescents were "terrorizing" the public school system of the United States. Which scenes in Parts One, Two, and Three of the novel (both in and out of the classroom and school building setting) do you think director Richard Brooks might have seized upon and highlighted to visualize this "terror" from so-called urban "juvenile delinquents"? Please be sure to also include your thinking as to whether the novel as a whole (and, by inference and association) the black-and-white film version of it, is truly "a novel of juvenile delinquents," as its 1954 cover stated.

4. When potential readers of the original pocket-book edition of the novel were asked to look at and read everything on the front cover of THE BLACKBOARD JUNGLE and then tell an interviewer what specifically they had seen on the cover, an overwhelming majority said that the buxom female was a student flirting with an available teacher and that the Black student was threatening the life of that teacher with an open switchblade knife. In terms of your experience with reading the novel and your knowledge of America's cultural history, talk about what you make of these misperceptions and misconceptions in the context of whether you think Evan Hunter not only set about to write

but also successfully achieved "a novel of juvenile delinquents," as its 1954 cover stated.

5. If you were making a new version of the 1955 film BLACKBOARD JUNGLE (with the "THE" or without the "THE" in your movie's title?), which three or four scenes from the novel would you take particular pains to "get right" (in terms of scripting, acting, directing, editing) so that your vision of the film (your thematic vision and your pictorial vision) would be sure to come across to a movie theater or home box office audience?

SO YOU THINK YOU MIGHT LIKE TO TEACH

Read all of Appendix "A" in Mr. Eidelberg's text on "The Education of Rick Dadier" (a compilation narrative of Rick Dadier's professional growth from all the SO YOU THINK YOU MIGHT LIKE TO TEACH chapter sections in which he is a featured player).

TEACHER MAN, a memoir by Frank McCourt

Read Chapter 7 of Mr. Eidelberg's text SO YOU THINK YOU MIGHT LIKE TO TEACH on "The Gift of Good Teaching" which features several remarkably good teachers at their best (so far!) in their classrooms. As you read, note where these "gifted" and "giving" teachers exhibit any of the good teaching traits and characteristics that former students in this course have found to be common to – and perhaps essential for – good teaching to take place. Expand their list to include any that you see demonstrated in Chapter 7 but not already stated (include those you believe that are implied but really need to be made explicit).

Begin your reading of Part III of Frank McCourt's novelized memoir TEACHER MAN. You are only responsible for studying Part III of this work, which is entitled "Coming of Age in Room 205"; please pace yourself to complete your reading of this final part of the memoir within the next four sessions. (If you have the time, interest, and inclination, go ahead and read Parts I and II on your own – they are quite well written.)

CW/HW
Please submit three sessions from now to both Mr. Eidelberg and your course partner an extended piece of cogent, coherent, and cohesive

writing in the form of **a personal and professional letter from you to Frank McCourt**, dealing with all or most of the following aspects of your reading experience.

In your opinion, does Frank McCourt become a "remarkable teacher," a memorable pedagogue who gives his students "the gift of good teaching"? If your answer is yes, explain how. If no, why not? Would you have wanted to be a student in his class when you were in high school (why or why not, and which specific high school was that, and where was it located)? And, if you are currently planning to become a teacher (or are already in the New York City school system in some way professionally), how does Frank McCourt serve as a kind of memoir mentor for you in his writing about "Coming Alive in Room 205" – or how does he fail to be a my-story mentor to you?

SESSION #9 OF THE TEACHER AND STUDENT IN LITERATURE ON REMARKABLE TEACHING AND LEARNING IN EVAN HUNTER'S NOVEL THE BLACKBOARD JUNGLE

Create, in writing at whatever length and in whatever tone of voice that works for your piece, ONE (just one, please) of the following "speech" options and email it to Mr. Eidelberg and your course partner. Choose wisely from the following five options, and select the detailed content, the structure, the attitude, and the writing style and voice that work best for you and for your insightful understanding of the novel and its various characters with respect to who and what constitutes "remarkable" teaching and learning.

1. Principal Small's testimonial speech to Richard Dadier (spoken at the last faculty only meeting of Rick's first year as a teacher at Manual Trades Vocational High School) in which Principal Small ("pal," not "ple") honors (or "honors") Mr. Richard Dadier for successfully completing his first year as a vocational high school English teacher;

2. The same occasion in space and time as Choice #1 but with the testimonial (or "testimonial") speech given by ONE of Rick's male or female teacher colleagues that past year at Manual Trades;

3. A "Teacher of the Year" Award speech at the end of Rick's first year teaching at Manual Trades (spoken by a particular student from the novel; identify him by name) who has volunteered to honor Rick before a gathering of faculty, students, and parents;

4. Rick's retirement-from-teaching speech after a 20-year-long long career in teaching (spoken from the heart to the assembled faculty

and staff of the school he finds himself teaching in when he decides it's time to retire);

5. A deeply felt (though perhaps self-deluded) letter to the student newspaper of North Manual Trades Vocational High School from one of the other teachers at the school explaining why they and NOT Rick Dadier should have been officially recognized as "remarkable" in the school newspaper's annual polling of students in the school.

FINE PRINT IMPORTANT NOTE: Pages 8 - 17 of Chapter 1 of STAYING AFTER SCHOOL feature a number of past CW/HW results for some of the above creative writing options; read these pages <u>before</u> you do any writing of your own only if you wish to experience how former students in this course approached the assignment (and eventually got their writing professionally published!); read these pages <u>after</u> you've done the first draft of your own piece of creative writing if you do not want to be unduly influenced beforehand by other students' approaches to the assignment. Or, if you prefer, by all means skip the information, ideas, and approaches on these pages entirely, and don't read them until after you have submitted your polished piece to Mr. Eidelberg and your course partner.

Here is teacher Rick Dadier's retirement speech as told in an "in-voice" piece of writing by Hunter College student Destiny Bolding:

I first want to thank everyone for coming and for everyone's kind words. Wow, twenty years - Daddy-Oh's been teaching for twenty years, who would have thought I'd last that long. You see, everyone always says life is a rollercoaster, I'd have to agree. In that case, my rollercoaster has been the most thrilling, yet nauseating one of all time - with the most drops, loopty-loops, and turns you could ever imagine. Some might say I should have gotten off many rides ago, but I did not. And why is that? Well, teaching has been the best thing that has ever happened to me and it has taken everything within me to walk away from this career.

But, I will not be leaving empty-handed. I will forever be accompanied by countless unforgettable memories - even the ones I've tried so hard to forget. From the good, the bad, and the ugly, teaching has shaped me into the man I have become today and for that I am eternally grateful. Grateful for all my successes, my failures, my students, and my colleagues. Teaching is not easy - it takes immense patience and dedication, but it is the most gratifying career there is, maybe I'm just being a little biased. As a teacher, you have a responsibility to serve, mentor, and guide your students and knowing you've made a positive mark on their lives is a feeling that is indescribable. But, I would like to take the time to acknowledge the mark my students have imprinted on my life. I will take the memories and lessons you all have taught me and hold them very close to my heart for the rest of my life. I could not have done it without my students. No, seriously, who would I be a teacher to if I didn't have them.

To everyone out there, never give up. If there is one thing to take away from my speech, I hope it is this. When you fall, get back up – never give up. If you have a goal, go for it. The sky's the limit. Throughout my career as a teacher, I cannot begin to count the amount of times I was faced with hardship – that is life. But, I cared too much about my job and students to ever give up on them. If you are going to do something, make sure to do it with every single bit of your heart. To all students, whether future teacher, astronaut, doctor, lawyer, or whatever your heart's desire: when you are knocked down, do not be discouraged. To my fellow teachers, never give up on your students and never give up on yourself. Keep fighting. Had I not done this, I would not be standing here today.

They say all good things in life must come to an end, and I guess this is the end. I guess it's time to put down the chalk and pick up a cane. Or as some of my students would probably tell me "time to start touring nursing homes, teach!" It is incredibly bittersweet to close this chapter of my life, but I am apprehensive to see what the future holds. Although I am unsure where the world will take me, I am sure of one thing. I will endlessly value my time as a teacher.

I would like to close off by giving thanks to those that made these memories happen. I would first like to thank my friends and family for their unconditional love and support outside of the classroom. I would also like to thank my bosses for believing in my abilities and providing me with the opportunity to teach. Next, my adored colleagues – thank you for guiding me and being my shoulder to cry on and more importantly, telling me all the gossip in the teacher's break room. And last, but certainly not least, I would like to thank each and every one of my students throughout my twenty-year span as a teacher. You all have molded me into the man I am today both in and out of the classroom. It is with great pride and gratitude that I reflect on my career on this stage, but the time has now come for me to walk away. It has been a long run but I am pleased to have made it through the blackboard jungle. Thank you all.

Here is student Gregory Miller's testimonial to teacher Rick Dadier as told in an "in-voice" piece of writing by Hunter College student Khadiza Sultana:

Well, what d'you know. If someone tole me in the beginning of the year that I'd be standin' here making a speech for Mr. Dadier – a "Teacher of the Year" award at that – I'd have said, "Hell, is he goan survive that long?" An' yere you are Chief; you survived this blackboard jungle. Must say I'm proud of you for holdin' on this entire year. Sure wasn' an easy road to take when we were given' you a hard time. Ain't that right fellers?

Joke aside, I'm glad you're yere Chief. Back then, I tole teach that I couldn't see anybody takin' the hard way when the easy way's open – that I needed someone to prove it to me. I wasn' sure of what I wanted to be in the future, an' even now, I don't have everythin' figured out. But I know now that whatever I decide on, I shunt just take the easy way out. Sure, it'll be hard, but hell, if Chief can be a hero for us, why can't I? Why can't I swim against the tide – to be a hero, even if it's just for myself?

So this is for Mr. Dadier, the teacher who made a dump heap a lil cleaner. The teacher who showed us that without a magic word, we can still fight dragons. The teacher who wants to teach and has done a pretty dammed good job at it. Here's to Mr. Dadier: Congrats Chief.

SESSION #10 OF THE TEACHER AND STUDENT IN LITERATURE ON THE 1955 HOLLYWOOD MOVIE VERSION OF EVAN HUNTER'S NOVEL THE BLACKBOARD JUNGLE

On YouTube, view director Richard Brooks's 1955 film version of Evan Hunter's 1954 novel THE BLACKBOARD JUNGLE. If you have been expecting an assignment to write a personal review of the film as both a movie viewer and a knowledgeable reader of the novel that inspired it, that is not quite Session #10's assignment, although the writing you will be doing will of course depend on how insightful you have been in your reading and viewing.

So here is the CW/HW actually triggered by a question one of you sent me about the making of the film: did Evan Hunter have any input into the writing and directing of "Blackboard Jungle" inspired by his novel THE BLACKBOARD JUNGLE?

In what I think of as an "in-voice" piece of creative and analytical writing, in this CW/HW you are not you directly; instead, you are the writer Evan Hunter and you, to answer that student's question, had absolutely no input - truly! - into the making of the film "Blackboard Jungle." Like your many readers, however, you were extremely curious as to what director Richard Brooks would do WITH and TO your novel. And now you know because it is 1955 and you have just seen the movie in a New York City movie house.

Some specific things in your novel that Brooks has kept (and the way he has depicted them) please you; some other things that Brooks has changed, modified, left out or added annoy or anger you; some of Brooks's directorial decisions even puzzle and confuse you. So, you're a writer;

what are you going to do with these thoughts and feelings and opinions of yours? Easy, you (and, remember, you are Evan Hunter) are going to write a personal letter to director Richard Brooks, a letter of specific pleasure and praise, a letter of particular confusion and complaint, a letter of both "thank-you" and "how-could-you!"

IMPORTANT NOTE: your personal letter as Evan Hunter must be true to your insightful novel-reading and film-viewing as a student in English 25147. So, feel free when writing as Evan Hunter, author and movie-goer, to consider and comment on any of the following aspects (plus any others you can think of): casting choices, performances by particular featured and supporting actors, plot changes, character modifications, downplaying or up-playing (magnifying) of any of the novel's themes, viewpoints, archetypes, and stereotypes, the film's story arc, plot line, and pacing, its use of black and white instead of color, its use of music on the soundtrack, notable and noticeable directorial decisions, notable and noticeable editing options and choices, significant script modifications, changes, additions, and subtractions (from the diction choices and sequencing that Hunter originally created). As another one of our longer novels (to be studied near the end of the semester) proclaims: Let this be a challenge to you. But also, have great intellectual fun with it!

Here are the opening paragraphs of author Evan Hunter's "review letter" to director Richard Brooks on Brooks's film version of Hunter's novel (through an "in-voice" piece of writing by Hunter College student Mahajabin Chowdhury):

Dear Richard Brooks,

I have recently viewed your film "Blackboard Jungle" based on my novel THE BLACKBOARD JUNGLE and I have to say that I am ambivalent as to how I should feel towards your adaptation. Although I do want to thank you for choosing this story about the American system of education for screening by cinema viewers, I want you to know that I am addled by particular parts of my novel that you decided to change or leave out.

Most of the film stayed true to what the moral of my novel is but small yet crucial parts are noticeably different. One of these is the relationship between Mr. Dadier and Miller. In my book these two different characters start at completely opposite ends, where Millar is the troubled student with no respect for adults and Richard Dadier is the teacher who struggles to get his vocational high school students to realize the importance of an education. There were multiple encounters between them, where Rick tried to guide Miller and show him the potential he has. It wasn't until the middle of the book that Miller shows a different side to his behavior. I made sure that these encounters were detailed and lengthy to show the progression of a teacher and student relationship building. The film, unfortunately, did not accurately portray the events between Richard and Miller – the encounters were brief and, towards the end of the film, the two suddenly became close. It seems that the relationship was rushed to get to the end, where they did bond, and even that was embellished to make them seem like they became best friends.

An example of this would be the scene you included where the two make a pact for Rick to continue teaching and Miller to continue being a student and not drop out. In my opinion, if the conversations were more intimate, as they were in the novel, the pact would have been redundant, but even the way it is, the scene seems to be arbitrary because there is no growth in the contact between them. And the scene of the Christmas show production, which was meant to show the change in the way these two characters saw each other, was too brief to have the intended impact. In fact, overall change in teacher and student perspectives was imprecise because the reality is that understanding and respect is gained through time and effort, and the film failed to show the effort Mr. Dadier put into gaining his students' cooperation.

Sincerely,

Evan Hunter

Here is how Hunter College student Danny Jiang approached the challenges and opportunities of adapting Evan Hunter's novel THE BLACKBOARD JUNGLE for the screen:

If I were to adapt THE BLACKBOARD JUNGLE into a new movie for 2020, I would include the "the" in the title of my movie. I believe that Evan Hunter included "the" in his title in order to emphasize how Manual Trades (and the vocational school system) is emblematic of "blackboard jungles." Though there may be other schools, academic or vocational, which can be called "blackboard jungles," the novel is a story about Rick's teaching experience in Manual Trades – his journey into the belly of the beast, or as Hunter puts it, "into the blackboard jungle without even knowing how many teeth there were in a lion's mouth" (Hunter, 149). Including "the" within the title of my movie serves to reinforce that Manual Trades is *the* Manual Trades.

For my adaptation of THE BLACKBOARD JUNGLE, there are a number of key scenes from the novel which I want to "get right," meaning that my interpreted reading of the novel must be combined with my interpretation of how Hunter envisioned the scenes in his novel. The first scene I would focus in on will be based on the events which occur at the end of chapter three. The chapter revolves around Rick obtaining his status here at Manual Trades. At the end of the chapter, the unclear status of hero is cemented in the sequence of decisions Rick makes at the end of his sixth-period class with 55 – 206. This sequence of events is important because it establishes the conflict between Rick and the blackboard jungle of Manual Trades. Rick (and the audience) do not yet know that being marked as a hero means the opposite - to be marked as a villain at Manual Trades, and the book emphasizes how a number of small decisions could have changed the outcome of Rick being labeled as a hero. For this scene, I would take care to note how Rick obtained his status at Manual Trades because he had chosen to leave the building instead of going to the teacher's lunchroom, to call the elevator and take the staircase because it didn't arrive, and to choose to follow the up and down signs on the staircases instead of continuing down the up staircase he was currently on. To emphasize this limbo-like state of Rick's unassigned sixth period, I would consider having two versions of the scene play out in tandem in a split-screen, with one side showing Rick's decisions, and the other showing the what-ifs.

The next scene I would like to focus on is the smashing of Josh's records. This scene was one of the most emotional scenes in the novel for me. Josh's despair drove home the indifference prevalent in Manual Trades, the "blackboard jungle" that it is. The lack of respect from the students for the teachers, and vice versa, creates an environment where there is no system of support or care. When Josh attempts to introduce his music to his class, all his records are shattered by his students. When I read the scene, I pictured the destruction of his vinyl happening in slow motion. I would also keep the frame of the scene especially tight, to establish a sense of claustrophobia and chaos amid "the records tumbling from their slots, falling like black rain, crashing against the floor, shattering, singly spattering the case thudding to the floor, too" (Hunter, 191).

Finally, I would like to focus on "the day Rick broke through," which was December 21, two days before the Christmas assembly, and also the day Anne went into labor. This day is important to the novel because it shows Rick being so close to obtaining his goal throughout the novel – to break through to his students and be respected as a teacher at Manual Trades – only to have it swept from him. Because Anne went into labor, Rick was unable to teach his breakthrough lesson to 55 – 206, his most problematic class. In addition, because his son was stillborn, Rick was unable to attend the Christmas Assembly which he and Miller had worked hard on. Emphasizing this scene would tie the idea of "what-if" back to the first scene I chose to get right. Rick as a character often makes choices he regrets, and stumbles into success. Not a lot of information is disclosed to the reader about what happens during the Christmas Assembly. For the movie adaptation, I would take care to include a scene of the assembly itself, even if Rick is absent from it. Particularly the end of the assembly, in which Miller's group of angels prepared a tie for Rick, is especially poignant. It shows us that Miller has come around to respect Rick – though he is not there to receive it. I would like to contrast the joys of Rick making his breakthrough and the joys of the Christmas assembly with the tragic stillbirth of Rick's son, by first showing his class, then Rick's time at the hospital, and finally the Christmas Assembly as Rick stays at home for a week.

SESSION #11 OF THE TEACHER AND STUDENT IN LITERATURE ON THE 1967 FILM "TO SIR, WITH LOVE" AND WHETHER IT IS A BRITISH "BLACKBOARD JUNGLE"

SO YOU THINK YOU MIGHT LIKE TO TEACH

Read the sections in Chapters 1, 3, 4, 5, and 7 of Mr. Eidelberg's text SO YOU THINK YOU MIGHT LIKE TO TEACH that examine the start of the teaching career of E. R Braithwaite in his novelized memoir TO SIR, WITH LOVE.

Or, **read** all of Appendix "B" in Mr. Eidelberg's text SO YOU THINK YOU MIGHT LIKE TO TEACH on "The Education of E.R. Braithwaite" (a sequential compilation narrative of Braithwaite's professional growth and development from all the SO YOU THINK YOU MIGHT LIKE TO TEACH chapter sections in which he is a featured player).

View free on YouTube the trailer to the film version of the novel TO SIR, WITH LOVE.

Or, **view free on YouTube** the entire film "To Sir, With Love," which stars Sidney Poitier in the role of the E.R. Braithwaite character (now called "Mark Thackeray"). Interesting fact: in this 1967 film Poitier plays a challenged Black teacher in an urban diverse British school; twelve years earlier he played the student Gregory Miller in the urban all-male American vocational high school in the 1955 film "Blackboard Jungle."

A Pair of Prompts:

Choice "A": It has been said that that E. R. Braithwaite in his novelized memoir TO SIR, WITH LOVE is the British version of the American newbie teacher Richard Dadier in Evan Hunter's novel THE BLACKBOARD JUNGLE. Without going essay-crazy (I mean it!) on this much too comprehensive question, choose *two or three key points* that you would make if you were on a debate team assigned this question of whether the story of TO SIR, WITH LOVE is the British version of THE BLACKBOARD JUNGLE (do your best to either shoot this argument down or to give it a boost up).

Choice "B": in an "in-voice" piece of writing, pretend you are the renowned actor Sidney Poitier writing his memoirs and, in one chapter of that book, looking back on a film-acting career in the 1950's and '60s and thinking about how acting as a student in the film "Blackboard Jungle" and later as a teacher in the film "To Sir, With Love" constituted "teaching moments" for him.

Here is how Hunter College student Victoria Cecere approached her writing of actor Sidney Poitier's memoir:

There is a lot to learn, know, and understand as you navigate throughout life. Note, there are significant differences between all three. Each possesses its own unique set of challenges – and each has its own reward. I feel as though people will be lost without all three. In order to understand my life, as well as the roles I chose, you will need to understand these three words and what they mean to me.

You can only learn so much, especially before your neural pathways "close." However, what you decide to learn in that span is completely up to you. For me, learning to act was my way of satisfying my need for knowledge. I learned how to conduct myself, and how to fill the shoes of others so I could conduct myself according to their standards. I've acted in a lot of different movies, with many different styles of learning featured in them.

However, the two I significantly appreciate were my roles in "Blackboard Jungle" and "To Sir, With Love." I had to learn a lot about both roles. Not only regarding the culture and language surrounding the films, but about the characters themselves. I had to learn about what motivated them. For

Gregory Miller in "Blackboard Jungle" it was an "unattainable" passion, and for Mark Thackeray in "To Sir, With Love," it was the need to teach his students so he did not have to find another job. I had to learn about how they would conduct themselves, and how they would act off script. I had to assess how they would deal with many situations.

I want to say that these roles helped me conduct myself a bit better. But these roles did teach me a lot about what was still to be learned and understood regarding racism. I got to fill two roles that were both the same and different, as both men struggled with their own identify at some point during the films. For Thackeray, it was when no students would be allowed near his home out of fear of rejections from others. For Miller, it was during one of his fights with the teacher Rick Dadier, when he realized that Dadier might have been "just like the others." I know what I've experienced during my lifetime, and I know what they have experienced by playing these roles. Both roles, although possibly controversial for their time, managed to touch on the topic of racism in a way that let others see what it was like in the shoes of others. I hope people did learn from these characters, as I thought I portrayed them very well.

I also learned a lot more about knowing and understanding people when filling these roles. Gregory Miller had to know and understand Dadier and his tricks in order to help pacify the classroom. I saw this during the scenes right before the fight with the student Arthur West, where Miller started to open up a bit to Dadier and help him out. For Thackeray, his entire role was focused on knowing and understanding his students (as well as the way they learned) in order to serve them better. If Thackeray had decided to quit and not learn and understand his students and their circumstances, there would have been no movie to produce!

Without these characters taking the time to know and understand other characters, these movies would not have done as well as they did. It was a learning experience for me, as I got to know and understand my fellow actors. I got to learn all their tiny tricks and quirks when changing roles and practicing lines. It was a learning experience on both sides of the spectrum and I'm glad to have been cast in both movies. Although I don't have the energy at my age to continue to act, I still have the ability to learn, know, and understand others, as well as the world around us. However, these roles were some of the best in teaching me that there is still so much more to learn and uncover.

Here is how Hunter College student Lisa Baez approached her writing of actor Sidney Poitier's memoir:

Looking back at the roles I played in the two films "Blackboard Jungle" and "To Sir, With Love," I decided to gauge myself on how far I reached with regards to the values and standards I set on myself back then. In this wonderful memoir, I explore my role as an iconic Afro-Bahamian actor. Throughout my life, I give credit to my parents for helping me create a sense of right and wrong as well as knowing my self-worth. Lessons on good and evil laid the foundation of a career as an actor. For the reason, I strived to attain all my set standards without surrender. In the film "Blackboard Jungle" I played the role of Gregory Miller, one of the delinquent students at school. While at school, I was one of the students who was eager to learn. But I must admit, I was not self-motivated nor did I have anyone who could motivate me until I met the remarkable teacher Richard Dadier. Richard Dadier was the new teacher in the school who witnessed the attempted rape of his female colleague, Miss Hammond. Dadier managed to reach out to me convincing me to abandon any negative thoughts as well as to believe in myself because I had high academic potential. Nonetheless, I believe that playing the role Gregory Miller was not as difficult as I could have imagined. I believe it was easy for me because this role was like a presentation of myself back when I was in school. I grew up in poverty to parents who worked as farmers. I had little formal education and was surrounded by violence. However, I can say that like Miller I wanted to become successful in life regardless of my misbehavior. In the film, I also acted as hope to the end of violence that heavily threatened the education system in the urban schools. In 1967, I managed to act in another film entitled "To Sir, With Love." In this film, I act as a remarkable teacher.

Despite the unruly behavior within students that forces many teachers to resign, I maintain my standards always reprimanding the misconduct from the students regardless of their emotions towards me. This scenario occurs when I diffused a fight between Potter and Mr. Bell. Mr. Bell is the gym teacher who loses some student support in the process of this fight. Despite all that, I ordered Potter to apologize to his gym teacher regardless of the wrongs committed bringing out the values I stood for in life. The elderly in society deserved respect, a virtue instilled in me by my parents. My role in "To Sir, With Love" shows to never give up on your students because one day you are going to get through to them giving them full motivation and guides. Despite my bad behavior and way of thinking in "Blackboard Jungle," I managed to reinstate my values of acting in the right way in the film "To Sir, With Love." In both movies, I managed to distinguish between the right and wrong actions. As a student, I displayed the bad behavior in students before correcting such behavior in the other film as a teacher. Without any doubt, the two films played a great role in portraying the values I stood for on good and evil as instilled by my parents.

BONUS SESSION OF THE TEACHER AND STUDENT IN LITERATURE ON MIND GAMES STUDENTS AND TEACHERS PLAY

SO YOU THINK YOU MIGHT LIKE TO TEACH

Read all of Chapter 5 in SO YOU THINK YOU MIGHT LIKE TO TEACH

Prompt:
How are these teachers in schools that are right or wrong for them? What factors contributed to the good matches and the bad matches (mismatches)?

SO YOU THINK YOU MIGHT LIKE TO TEACH

Read all of Chapter 3, which is inspired by Eric Berne's 1960's non-fiction work GAMES PEOPLE PLAY. SO YOU THINK YOU MIGHT LIKE TO TEACH applies Berne's work to the *psychological* mind games *that students and teachers play with and against each other* (in such novels as THE DEAD SCHOOL; TO SIR, WITH LOVE; HARD TIMES; and THE BLACKBOARD JUNGLE)

Prompt:
Of the many teacher-student mind games discussed in Chapter 3, which is your favorite one – and why (the one you are just dying to share your thoughts about with your course partner)?

STAYING AFTER SCHOOL

As a foundation for the creative writing assignment coming up next, read all of Chapter 4 (pages 31 - 42) in STAYING AFTER SCHOOL; the chapter contains several published examples of psychological mind games played by students and teachers (all from the experiences as well as the imaginations of former Hunter College students of Mr. Eidelberg).

CW/HW CREATIVE WRITING ASSIGNMENT

Create a psychological mind game that teachers and students have been known to play with each other or, in your fertile imagination, might conceivably play in the classrooms of the future; fully describe the opposing goals, strategies, tactics, and operations of such a game.

Or, if you are up to the challenge, create your psychological mind game as an ACTUAL "PARKER BROTHERS"-type BOARD GAME fitted out with playing board; moving pieces; chance, risk, and opportunity cards; and so on. But it absolutely must be a kind of "mind" game. You might, early on, want to send by email a draft of your mind game to your course partner to get revision feedback on how to make your game more playable.

Here is how Hunter College student Shelly Uzagir responded to the academic and creative challenges of this bonus session on classroom mind games:

How are these teachers in Chapter 5 in schools that are either right or wrong for them? What factors contributed to the good matches and the bad matches (mismatches)?

Sy Levin was at the wrong school. Although he advised he would be happy at any college out west, he certainly was not aware of the position he had accepted. The factor that contributed to his bad match is that he did not have a job interview therefore, he was unable to ask questions about the position/school. Rick Dadier of THE BLACKBOARD JUNGLE had an interview similar to Sy Levin's but he did not obtain information about the school and was unaware of whether or not it was the right match. Braithwaite did receive insight into his school, unsolicited, but insight nonetheless. In addition, he was also able to wander around the building and inspect the school prior to accepting the teaching position. Therefore, Braithwaite was given a transparent idea of the school and he was able to determine if it was a match for him. Although he predicted the position would be temporary, I do believe it was the right match. Tom Mason was employed at a particularly strange school (or at a strange time); therefore, I don't think the high school where a murder occurred was the right match for him, or any teacher for that matter. A significant factor is inquiring about the school, faculty and students when the teacher begins his/her employment. I think the questions included in the chapter are wonderful to ask one's self when trying to determine if they've found their match. In regards to Dan Elish's experience, I surely could not imagine going back to my high school as a teacher. Don't get me wrong, I enjoyed my experience as a student; however, I remember how badly the teachers were treated.

Conversely, I understand wanting to go back and make/be the difference that is so desperately needed. The important factor is simply understanding the why behind wanting to work at the particular school. There is also nothing wrong with experiencing the school, even if you feel it is temporary. One thing I've learned from reading about these teachers' experiences is that their school was not their first or ideal choice, it was not their matches, but they found purpose there.

Of all the many teacher-student mind games discussed in Chapter 3, which is your favorite one – and why (which are you just dying to share your thoughts about with your course partner)?

The "Resistance to a New Teacher" teacher-student mind game is an oldie, but a goodie. As I was reading the commentary on this game, I reflected on a time in ninth grade when my teacher went on maternity leave one month prior to summer vacation. Our class was assigned a new, young teacher who undoubtedly could've passed for a student. Perhaps if it was mid-semester the students would've attempted to work with her, but Regents had already been completed and final grades had already been calculated. She tried to be authoritative, she did not hesitate to raise her voice or threaten to give us extra homework. However, the students ultimately won the game. There was no co-operation; therefore, no teaching or learning. Everyone, including the teacher, was simply waiting for the time to run out and freshman year to come to an end. "Resistance to a New Teacher" is my favorite mind-game because I'm familiar with it. However, it's risky because students can choose to rebel by simply disobliging. Without combined effort from the teacher and students, there is not learning. Instead, I would recommend appealing to students' interests, building transparency and being genuine, because believe it or not, students can see through the tough-guy act.

Create a psychological mind game that teachers and students have been known to actually play with each other or, in your fertile imagination, might conceivably play in the classrooms of the future; fully describe the opposing goals, strategies (overall plans for winning), tactics (moves), and operations of such a game. (Optional: You might, early on, want to send a draft of your mind game to your course partner to get revision feedback for your finished version of the mind game based on your partner's telling you by email what they consider to be the draft's strengths and weaknesses as a playable game.)

To be truthful, I am not partial to teachers playing psychological mind games with students. It could be the naive, unexperienced teacher in me that believes there should be a clear, sole purpose of teaching and learning in the classroom. However, I am aware that mind games may be necessary in certain schools with reluctant students. I just felt the need to express my opinion on the matter. If I were to create a mind game that teachers have been known to actually play with students, it would be called "divide and conquer." In fact, Rick Dadier attempted a similar tactic when he tried to gain the trust and obedience of Gregory Miller. Usually, the teacher attempts to win over the most rebellious student who was often the kingpin of the classroom. If the teacher was successful in the game, the student would accept the teacher. Even if the other unruly students were not initially fond of the teacher, they eventually followed suit. Like any "divide and conquer" strategy, the goal was to gain control over the classroom leader in order to separate them from their followers, to prevent them from uniting in opposition against the teacher. The moves include assigning the student favorable tasks, such as handing out the textbooks, erasing the chalk board and taking the basketballs out of the storage closet for recess (that required the student to leave the classroom a couple minutes prior to the bell ringing). This sort of preferential treatment would not leave time for the student to be disruptive and will certainly put the teacher in their good graces. Another tactic is reassuring the student that they are extremely bright and charged with potential, a compliment they may not have received from teachers in the past because they weren't able to look past the misbehavior. This mind-game almost surely works because children are easily influenced by their peers.

SESSION #12 OF THE TEACHER AND STUDENT IN LITERATURE ON FRANK MCCOURT'S 2004 MEMOIR TEACHER MAN

TEACHER MAN by Frank McCourt

Now that you have finished your reading of and thinking about Part III of Frank McCourt's novelized memoir, please submit an extended piece of writing-**a personal and professional letter from you to Frank McCourt** – dealing with all or most of the following aspects of your reading experience.

In your opinion, does Frank McCourt become a "remarkable teacher," a memorable pedagogue who gives his students "the gift of good teaching"? If your answer is yes, explain how. If no, why not? Would you have wanted to be a student in his class when you were in high school (why or why not, and which specific high school was that, and where was it located)? And, if you are currently planning to become a teacher (or are already in the New York City school system in some way professionally), how does Frank McCourt serve as a kind of memoir mentor for you in his writing about "Coming Alive in Room 205" – or how does he fail to be a my-story mentor to you?

What do you think about Hunter College student Danny Jiang's response to whether Frank McCourt was a remarkable teacher at Stuyvesant High School?

SOME DAY I PLAN TO BE THE CHAIR OF THE ENGLISH DEPARTMENT AT NEW YORK CITY'S STUYVESANT HIGH SCHOOL – THE HIGH SCHOOL WHERE TEACHER MAN FRANK MCCOURT TAUGHT CREATIVE WRITING

Dear Mr. McCourt,

I plan on finding myself in your shoes someday. I went to Stuyvesant, though not the one you knew – I attended Stuyvesant in the new building, after the school moved from 14th Street to lower Manhattan in Tribeca. Though you may have thought you weren't qualified to teach, in the end you became a truly remarkable teacher, and your legacy lives on at Stuyvesant. You're something of a legend in the halls, especially on the sixth floor, where the library and English classrooms are. I'm almost positive that every freshman or sophomore reads your novel ANGELA'S ASHES at some point in the school year. Any English teacher will make sure to tell the students that you've taught there. Creative Writing is still offered every year, and still just as oversubscribed as it was when you began teaching it—and each student takes the class because they want to write, not for the "easy A" which you thought to be the reason.

It was my journey through the English Department at Stuyvesant that solidified my wish to return there and teach. Looking back, I realize that many of the things I took for granted in my classes at Stuyvesant can be traced back to your time there. I take immense pride in my identity as a Stuyvesant alumnus, and Stuyvesant students pride themselves on the breadth of courses they have access to. It's within these courses that the remnants of your creative teaching practices live on. I'm able to remember my teacher bringing in madeleines and tea for our study of Proust, because of your recipe musicals and banquets in the park.

It's enduring and comforting to know that the Stuyvesant I hold fondly in my memory is the same one you hold in TEACHER MAN. Your "Coming Alive in Room 205" reflects my own awakening as a lover of literature in the new building, in Room 615A. Now, I think back to all the times I walked past the Museum Room in the new building, a "Room 205" (funnily enough, the room is on the second floor of the new building) which serves as a time capsule, preserving the history of Stuyvesant's classrooms in the old location a few blocks uptown. I think that this process of coming alive in a classroom is exactly what becoming a remarkable teacher entails.

To claim your classroom as a living extension of yourself, to me, means that you have achieved "remarkability" as a teacher: you, as a person, your curriculum, and your physical space come together and form the basis of a person that is passionate about what they have to say and teach. I especially liked that you claim yourself to not be a "teacher" of Creative Writing, because you admit that you are always learning. This is something I want to hold myself to as well. It's also something I hold to be a hallmark of a "remarkable" teacher: someone who isn't really a teacher at all, but rather a lifelong student of their work and their students' work.

I am lucky to have taken your class, in a way, because I was lucky to attend the school you taught at. And I consider myself lucky to be pursuing the career you found yourself in, because it's clear that you have a natural gift for it. Creative Writing is also the type of writing I want to teach, as you taught it: unconventionally and unapologetically. For me to become a remarkable teacher, I know that I must strive to become the teacher you were.

Danny Jiang

Hunter College

SESSION #13 OF THE TEACHER AND STUDENT IN LITERATURE ON THE TONE OF THE TWO-WORD TITLE TEACHER MAN

How do you say (out loud) the two-word title of Frank McCourt's novelized memoir? When in past terms I have taught this work of literature in a course of mine, I made a point of never (and it wasn't easy) saying its title out loud. Instead, I would refer to the memoir as the "Frank McCourt book." Of course, my students thought I was being weird (more weird than usual, that is), but I would tell them that there was, to paraphrase the play HAMLET, a method to my madness.

Pan to the pandemic and all of you connected to me by a line that is "on"; this semester I could walk around my home in Brooklyn saying the title TEACHER MAN aloud dozens of times and none of you, my non-Zoom students, would be the wiser. (But isn't being "the wiser" a large part of why we are connected?) So, how would you say the two words TEACHER MAN to me, to us, or out loud to yourself if you wanted to not only to be heard but to be understood correctly?

Huh? What's to understand? Here's what to understand: a dozen possible ways to say the title of this Frank McCourt book so that the sound, and the tone of voice, and the rhythm, and pacing, and the emphasis of those two words (perhaps indicated or helped along by punctuation marks) all accurately and fully convey what McCourt meant when he chose that particular title. (By the way, there are no such problems or opportunities with another two-word McCourt title, ANGELA'S ASHES.)

So, as Frank McCourt (since this is an "in-voice" writing assignment), which of the following possibilities do you consider absolutely wrong, which could be accepted as right, and which, when it comes right down to it, is the way you, Frank McCourt, meant the sound and meaning of your title to be? Please frame your response and its reasons as a letter from Frank McCourt to high school English teachers everywhere.

1. Teacher, Man (the way Joe Biden said directly to Donald Trump, "C'mon, man")
2. Teacher, Man (a teacher as well as a man)
3. Teacherman (all three syllables pretty much equally stressed)
4. Teacherman (as a putdown, "garbageman")
5. Teacher, *Man (a wow, about him)*
6. Teacher, *Man (oh man, a measly teacher)*
7. Teachermun (the last syllable is swallowed)
8. Teacher, Man!
9. Teacher? Man.
10. Teacherman! (Superman!)
11. Teacherman?
12. Teacher! Man

Here is how Hunter College student Rifath Islam filed her "in-voice" piece of writing with her pronounced opinions on how to say out loud the title of Frank McCourt's memoir:

To All High School English Teachers:

As many of you must know, the purpose of writing my book TEACHER MAN was to emphasize the struggles of being a teacher, alongside the benefits that come with taking such a position. In my book, you all saw the way I turned the events of my experience as a teacher into a memoir, and it may have elicited many different responses, as is expected. There is the possibility of reading my book and perhaps re-evaluating the decision of being a teacher, because could it possibly be that hard? Or it could have evoked a response of "Wow, this is tough, but a role I'm ready to take on." Regardless, I think many of the reactions are also tied into *how* the title of this memoir is pronounced.

I have heard many different pronunciations, among them some good, some bad, some maybes, and the way I intended it. Those pronunciations I absolutely did not intend were the following:

- Teacher, Man (the way Joe Biden said directly to Donald Trump, "C'mon, man")

- Teacherman (as a putdown, like saying "garbageman")
- Teacher, *Man* (*oh man, a measly teacher*)
- Teachermun (the last syllable is swallowed)

The problem with these four pronunciations is that they all seem to have a negative connotation behind them about the position of a teacher. Though, no, I truly was not trying to "toot my own horn" as a teacher in writing this memoir, but the purpose of it was to ensure that readers should see that the role of teachers in general should be appreciated more.

Other pronunciations that evoke a "maybe" from me are:

- Teacher, Man!
- Teacher? Man.
- Teacherman?
- Teacher! Man.

These pronunciations are, again, not necessarily wrong. However, the way I wrote the title, I had envisioned words as separate entities, with more of a heroic emphasis placed on the words. Therefore, the most likely pronunciations I would have intended were:

- Teacherman (all three syllables pretty much equally stressed)
- Teacher, *Man* (*a wow, about him*)
- Teacherman! (Superman!)

These pronunciations most clearly emphasize that the role of the teacher is something that is to be admired, which is essentially the idea that I was hoping to achieve in writing this through the title.

That being said, I think this would be an interesting lesson to teach, both to gauge an understanding of how a student perceives their teacher (or even teachers in general), or to understand a student's understanding of the role of a teacher.

Best,

Frank McCourt
Teacher Man

SESSION #14 OF THE TEACHER AND STUDENT IN LITERATURE: HELLO TO THE 1934 NOVELLA GOODBYE, MR. CHIPS

GOOD-BYE, MR. CHIPS by James Hilton

Actually, it's "Hello, Mr. Chips" – and goodbye to those other remarkable teachers we've met so far

Read Chapters 1 – 10 in whatever edition you have (it's pages 4 - 34 in the quite inexpensive Acra edition, which doesn't number the 18 short chapters, but it's quite easy to see where each begins – maybe that's where Acra saved some money!)

Here's an extended prompt of academic writing to be sent to both Mr. Eidelberg and your course partner:

What are your first impressions of Mr. Chips and how do they compare with your last impressions of Rick Dadier of THE BLACKBOARD JUNGLE and Mark Thackeray of "To Sir, With Love"? Also, how is the structuring of this British novella (a novella is a short novel, usually around 100 or so pages) different from the structuring of the very much longer American novel THE BLACKBOARD JUNGLE – and what explains this distinction with a difference? How significant is this difference to the experience the reader of GOODBYE, MR. CHIPS has with the lives of the characters, the plot of the story, and the themes of the novella?

Here is part of how Hunter College student Dixiory Burgos Utate responded:

From the beginning of the book my first impression of Mr. Chips was that he was this old teacher who probably had an old teaching style that did not include interacting with the students. To me he was one of those teachers who did not care how the students received the materials they were learning; as long as they received them that was all that mattered. Richard Dadier, however, came off in the beginning of THE BLACKBOARD JUNGLE, as self-driven, a man who went into an interview with his head up high and speaking as clear as he could when asked a question. Mark Thackeray in the film "To Sir, With Love" started off his teaching job as a man who knew what he was getting himself into.

The major difference in how these teachers' stories was told in print is that Dadier's is told in the present tense by a narrator and Chips's story is told in the past tense by having a narrator have Chips recall his teaching days. Dadier had no idea what was to come from his new job at a vocational high school and this changes the experience of the story for the reader: we are going through the journey with Dadier. With Chips, the reader is looking back on the journey with him.

SESSION #15 OF THE TEACHER AND STUDENT IN LITERATURE ON JAMES HILTON'S 1934 NOVELLA GOODBYE, MR. CHIPS,

GOODBYE, MR. CHIPS

Read through to the end of the novella (Chapters 11 – 18, pages 35-64 in the Acra edition)

SO YOU THINK YOU MIGHT LIKE TO TEACH

Re-read a tiny bit about the novella GOODBYE, MR. CHIPS in Chapter 2 of Mr. Eidelberg's text SO YOU THINK YOU MIGHT LIKE TO TEACH (just pages 33 bottom to 34 bottom). You've already read these two pages in SO YOU THINK YOU MIGHT LIKE TO TEACH (it's where Rick Dadier of THE BLACKBOARD JUNGLE is quoted as saying in Evan Hunter's novel that Mr. Chips was "a nice enough old man" who was particularly interested in being loved," whereas he, Rick, wanted to be seen as "tough" because he was interested in doing the job of teaching and in being "respected" for that).

Prompts for brief academic writing (think about all four, but write about only two, and send them on to both Mr. Eidelberg and your course partner):

1. Now that you've actually met and come to know Mr. Chips as a man and as a teacher, how honest and accurate was Rick's characterization of Mr. Chips? Where – and how exactly – is Rick on target, or not?

2. Think back on the gender of the teachers – actual and fictional – that you have experienced in your life to date: what part, if any, did their gender play in these educators' teaching personas and educational philosophies?

3. Think back on this: What effect did meeting Katherine, marrying Katherine, and losing Katherine and their child have on Mr. Chips as a person, as a man, as a teacher?

4. Can you explain why so many older American readers of this British novella believed that its author, James Hilton, must have based the fictional Mr. Chips on an actual American (and not British) public school teacher they had had in an American secondary school? Try to explain this phenomenon by making A LIST of reasons why you think so many older Americans might have "recognized" Mr. Chips in this way.

Here is how Hunter College student Anika Bradley responded to Prompts #1 and #3 on Rick Dadier's characterization of Mr. Chips and of Mr. Chips' wife Katherine's remarkable effect on Mr. Chips as a teacher:

Prompt #1: Rick Dadier's characterization of Mr. Chips is completely inaccurate. Rick believes that Mr. Chips' goal was to become "beloved" in his teaching role but in James Hilton's novella it's clear that Mr. Chips' goal was to teach and pass on his knowledge. He wasn't trying to be beloved in the same way that he wasn't trying to be overly strict or harsh on the boys. Like any teacher, I'm sure, he wanted to be loved by his students; it would surely make the job easier for him, but he also wanted to be respected and obeyed in the classroom. Only once "obedience he had secured, and honor has been granted to him," could he develop a loving relationship betweeen teacher and students (Hilton 32). Because the boys were well-behaved in his classroom and paid attention, Mr. Chips was able to express more of his personality to the class, including his famous sense of humor. Rick said that Chips was a "nice old man" and because of that, he wasn't tough on his boys. But actually, it is the opposite. He didn't need to be tough because he had already earned the students' respect. He is loved because he loves his students right back and respects them as well. As Hilton shows through one of the headmasters, Ralston, the tough guy act is not enough to secure a productive relationship from your students. When Ralston tries to convince Chips to resign, the students just about have a revolt at the prospect of Mr. Chips being forced to leave. This unexpected reaction caused Chips to learn that Ralston "was thoroughly unpopular, he was feared and respected, but not liked, and in the issue of Chips the dislike rose to the point where it conqured fear and demolished even respect" (Hilton 70). Students are much more inclined to respect and listen to a teacher who returns the effort rather than be forced into submission by one who thrives off of power. Mr. Chips is weak-willed because he is nice and friendly, he is good teacher because of his two-way street dynamic with his students.

Prompt #3: Though they were not together long, Katherine played an integral role in Chips' life. Meeting and marrying her helped expand his view of the world as her views were much more progressive than his own. When she moves into Brookfield with him, the audience sees her progression and liveliness expand through not only their marriage but to the whole school as well. The sports game between the two schools that did not really get along much before and then became an annual tradition was all Katherine's idea. Mr. Chips' fellow staff members and his students all noticed the change in his personality and teaching as well. He came alive in their relationship and that spread throughout his whole life. He was lovable in the classroom and started telling jokes while he was teaching to make people laugh. Losing his unborn child and Katherine in the same day is devastating for Chips, but Hilton makes it clear to readers how much Kathie has passed away, but Chips holds on to that ability to make Mrs. Wickett and the other boys who come to sit with him laugh. He becomes known for his jokes and the school goes crazy swapping back and forth Chips' jokes. Even on his last day, he is making one of the boys, Linford, laugh while having tea together. Though Mr. Chips never had any biological children of his own, in his very last words, he proclaims he has thousands of kids, "all of 'em boys," indicating all the students he's grown to love over the years (Hilton 114). The loss of Kathie and his child were heartbreaking, but he did not let that loss overtake his life and he turned it around, continuing on in a way he knew Kathie would want him to.

SESSION #16 OF THE TEACHER AND STUDENT IN LITERATURE ON SAYING "GOODBYE" TO GOODBYE, MR. CHIPS

GOODBYE, MR. CHIPS

Read over the three choices (A, B, C, in the bold italic type on the next page) for the writing you will now be doing about GOODBYE, MR. CHIPS.

Decide which is your first choice and which is your second; then contact (via email or cellphone) your course partner to find out their first and second choices. Decide between the two of you which choice you will actually write about and which choice your partner will write about (the two of you cannot write about the same choice and, thus, one of the three choices will be cast aside).

To help both of you decide, look over the prompt questions (in bold italics) that Mr. Eidelberg would have asked the speaker of each choice had he been asked to do this assignment; for your background information, Mr. Eidelberg found these negative statements on the internet – and they were all made by recent young-ish American readers of GOODBYE, MR. CHIPS who read the book as either a high school English class assignment or on the recommendation of a parent who had read the novella decades ago and remembered it fondly.

After you have completed your piece of writing – in the form of a letter to the recent American reader (you are writing as a fellow recent reader of GOODBYE, MR. CHIPS) – exchange your piece of writing with your course partner, read theirs, and then write back a letter to your partner containing your thoughts, feelings, reactions, agreements, disagreements, etc. with what your partner's piece of writing said (your partner will, of course, be doing the exact same thing for you).

Last step, send your piece of writing (Choice A, B, or C) AND the written reaction of your partner to it to Mr. Eidelberg as the completion of all the written work for this session.

(A) "Boring, boring, boring. It wasn't very interesting, and all it talked about was this teacher and his life. Also, it's supposed to be funny, I think."

"A" prompts: Was it all that boring? Everywhere and all the time? What made it so boring? What else should it have talked about beside "this teacher and his life"? Also, what gave you the idea that the novella was supposed to be funny and, not so incidentally, how did you determine that the book failed in its attempts to be "funny"?

(B) "Mixed up in time, confusingly structured. Also, not at all heart-wrenching (the way I like the stories I read to be)."

"B" prompts: How mixed up in time – and so what? And was the mixed-up plot intentional or was the structural playing with time just bad writing? Never ever heart-wrenching? Is "heart-wrenching" what we always want to experience as readers of fiction?

(C) "Enough with all the British history and culture and all the boys always going off to war and saying goodbye to Mr. Chips! Also, hours of pointless details. The author has no apparent reason for writing this story."

"C" prompts: What, actually, would have been "enough" British history and culture and off-to-war taking leave of Mr. Chips? What points through specific details should the novella have been making that you believe it never made? No overall authorial purpose at all? At all?

Here is how Hunter College student Destiny Bolding responded to prompt "B" on how author James Hilton structured his novella *GOODBYE, MR. CHIPS:*

"B" prompts: How mixed up in time - and so what? And the mixed-up plot intentional or was the structural playing with time just bad

writing? Never ever heart-wrenching? Is "heart-wrenching" what we always want to experience as readers of fiction?

Dear fellow reader,

I am deeply saddened to hear that you were not pleased by GOODBYE, MR. CHIPS. It is truly unfortunate that you did not have an amazingly positive experience like I did alongside thousands of other readers but everyone is entitled to their opinions and I will try to objectively view your criticisms. I would be lying if I said I fully understood the time mixing of the plot instantly because I did not, and it did take me a while to get used to. There were instances where the narrator was talking about a close past and other times referred to a more distant past so I can see where you are coming from and I understand how this can make the plot a bit challenging to comprehend and confusing to someone. I would like to say the mixed-up plot was an intentional move made on the author's part. I am not quite sure why he did so, but I can say with confidence that this was *not* a bad writer – so it must have had some predetermined significance. "Never ever heart-wrenching"? I mean come on! With all due respect was it not heart-wrenching to see Mr. Chips grow old and sick and eventually witness him become so intensely lonely? I can confidently say there were moments of heart-wrench in this story. However, if you did not, that is okay too. Perhaps not everything has to be heart-wrenching as we do not always look for a fictional story to be heart-wrenching as we all have different tastes. But I cannot help but question your ability to not be moved by Mr. Chips' heart-wrenching story. It is unfortunate that you were unable to overlook your confusion and critiques to see the bigger picture of the beautiful novel that is GOODBYE, MR. CHIPS. Perhaps reading the story a second time around will grant you the clarification that is needed to view the book in a different light. However, once again, at the end of the day, we are all allowed to have our own thoughts and feelings about literature as it tends to be open for interpretation, and I respect your thoughts although I may disagree with some.

Respectfully,

Destiny Bolding

BONUS SESSION OF THE TEACHER AND STUDENT IN LITERATURE ON THE 1934 BRITISH (BUT UNIVERSAL?) MR. CHIPS AND HIS 1962 AMERICAN TELEVISION "TWILIGHT ZONE" VERSION

CW/HW on GOODBYE, MR. CHIPS

I am NOT requiring that you watch the full 1939 movie "Goodbye, Mr. Chips" because there no longer appears to be a free English-language version of it on YouTube (but "feel free" to rent it some time if you'd still like to see it). However, do take a look at the free trailer, which is noted for radio commentator Alexander Wolcott's introductory speech expressing his "fear" that the Sam Wood-directed film of GOODBYE, MR. CHIPS would not do justice to the iconic book he loves so much; the trailer also shows you how the British actor Robert Donat portrayed Mr. Chippings (and went on to win the very first Academy Award Oscar ever issued for best actor of the year in 1939). Other free YouTube stuff: the opening and closing scenes of the movie and Mr. Chips' retirement speech.

By my count there are four other film and television versions of James Hilton's acclaimed novel, including an absolutely unwatchable (in my opinion) 1969 movie musical version, which should have been called "Goodbye, Mr. Chips, and Hello, the Chippings" for its story of their romance, marriage, and joint career at Brookfield. You can rent that on YouTube, too, if you can't wait to see what "unwatchable" looks and sounds like. (Better yet is the unwatchable in microcosm: watch British singing-star Petula Clark belt out her songs in the free trailer!)

And now for the required YouTube viewing:
Find "The Changing of the Guard," a 1962 episode from the famous television anthology series "The Twilight Zone," and watch the four-minute black-and-white **YouTube clip** from it. What Rod Serling, the creator of "The Twilight Zone" series has done, is change Mr. Chips into an elderly and suicidal American college professor who, as he thinks back on his long career, muses on whether it was worth it, whether he accomplished anything of value with his life's work, and whether he has made any appreciable difference as a teacher.

Prompt (for writing to be sent to both Mr. Eidelberg and your course partner):
Write a letter to author James Hilton telling him (based on what you directly see and hear in this clip and indirectly from any inferences you can make) what Rod Serling has, in fact, kept from Hilton's original story, why probably and what you think of all that, as well as what Serling has changed from Hilton's original story, and why probably. Give your reasons for your feelings about these changes and, if you can, tell why you think James Hilton would have had trouble "recognizing" his novella after it has entered the dimension known as "the twilight zone."

Here is how Hunter College student Anika Bradley experienced "The Twilight Zone" version of James Hilton's novella:

Dear James Hilton,

Hello Mr. Hilton, I hope you're doing well. I've just watched the episode of the TV show "The Twilight Zone" from 1962 that I heard was based on the novella GOODBYE, MR. CHIPS. I enjoyed your book and am an aspiring teacher. I loved hearing about Mr. Chips' life and his love of teaching. The episode definitely gave off a very different feeling about Chips' attitude towards his career and I'm curious as to whether you've seen the episode and, if so, what you thought about it.

Mr. Chips' name is changed to Professor Fowler in the episode and the plot begins with Professor Fowler being forced to retire after 50 years of teaching at the all-boys school. Remind you of anything, Mr. Hilton? It is very reminiscent of the scene in your novella where Ralston tries to force Chips to retire but the boys of the school fall into an uproar about it (one of my favorite parts of the book). What takes place after this occurrence, however, is distinctly different from your book. Fowler goes home and grows more and more depressed about the situation making himself believe that his entire career has been worthless and he hasn't actually done any good for the boys he educated and has only wasted their time with "useless poetry" and dead languages. He believed he has done nothing for humanity and therefore has himself become useless. Sadly, Fowler grows very suicidal and takes a gun to the school, planning on killing himself in the middle of the night outside the building.

This certainly is a different version of Chips than readers see in your book, isn't it? Perhaps it's for the best that they changed his name to Fowler because the man behind the similar plotline is certainly no Mr. Chips from what I recall based on my recent reading. Chips never believed his career as an educator to have been a mistake even when Ralston was trying to coerce him into retiring. In fact, that event and his students' reaction only seem to make him *more* confident in his choices. Teaching seems to be the one thing Chips was never regretful or sorry about over the course of his life. Even after his eventual retirement he still loved his boys.

In the conclusion of the episode, Fowler is visited in his classroom by the ghosts of this former students who have passed away. They have come to tell him all that he meant to them and how he was the one that inspired them to show bravery or courage in their lives and when protecting others. As Fowler says in the end of the episode, he may not have been directly the one to do humanity justice, but he helped hundreds of others do that job themselves and therefore he has done his part for the world.

The visit from the former students reminded me of when Chips would be visited by the new student at the school or by his old students. The interaction it greatly reminds me of is when Chips runs into one of the boys who had played on one of the first visiting sports teams at Brookfield and they reminisce about Chips' wife together. The boy, now a soldier, died a month later in the war just like how all the boys in the episode are dead. They didn't know each other long but their few interactions, and the soldier's with Katherine, left such an imprint on both their lives that they could never forget each other, in life for Chips or in death for the soldier. When the boys in the episode were doing their duties to humanity, such as sacrificing their lives during Pearl Harbor to save innocents or receiving the Medal of Honor for deeds in Iwo Jima, they recalled their experiences with Fowler and the moments of his teachings that made them want to become better men.

What Rod Sterling is portraying is his episode 1962 "The Changing of the Guard" is something that I think Chips always believed he had - the power to change the lives of others and make the world a better place through knowledge. Fowler needed the visit from death to truly see what he has done for the world, while Chips saw it himself everyday in his life Katherine and his interactions with the boys before and after his retirement.

I believe that while you may not see much relation between Chips and Fowler, you would see a clear connection between the message of your story and the message of this episode, at least I did. Obviously, I can't speak for you, Mr. Hilton, which is why I am writing to you because I'd like to hear your opinion on the matter.

Sincerely,

Anika Bradley

SESSION #17 OF THE TEACHER AND STUDENT IN LITERATURE ON THE SCHOOLMARM IN LITERATURE AND ON THE 1955 HOLLYWOOD MOVIE "GOOD MORNING, MISS DOVE"

GOOD MORNING, MISS DOVE

Read in STAYING AFTER SCHOOL only pages 31 through almost the bottom of page 33; these pages depict a mind game played by pupil Angela Adams and her teacher in Frances Gray Patton's 1954 novel GOOD MORNING, MISS DOVE

Prompt due to Mr. Eidelberg and your course partner:
Where exactly did Angela Adams make the wrong tactical move in her game against Miss Dove, and how was that move so seriously wrong? Up to that point in this mind game, what had been Angela's probably-bound-to-win strategy? How do we as readers of the novel know that it is indeed Miss Dove who wins that particular game? (For some optional assistance to your thinking, read in STAYING AFTER SCHOOL from page 33 bottom to the next to the last paragraph on page 34.)

SCHOOLMARMS IN LITERATURE

The elementary school teacher you have just met – Miss Dove – is considered a schoolmarm. What current associations do you have when you read or hear that word? Scribble them down NOW before continuing. Ready? The word "schoolmarm" looks to be a combination of the word "school" and the word "marm." We have no problem with "school," but what is this word "marm"? Actually, "marm" is a contraction of the originally French word "madam." Can you see where the "d" in "madam" drops out, leaving "maam," which winds up being pronounced as though it was written as "marm," and, in short order, changes its spelling to correspond to how everyone is regularly saying the word? So, stop again and add to your scribbled list of your associations for the word "schoolmarm" some more, now that you know it is referring to a "school madam."

Here is Hunter College student Janel Fernandez's analysis of how student Angela Adams lost a student and teacher mind game and how her elementary school teacher, Miss Dove, won it:

As suggested in your prompt I read the dialogue twice. It definitely made a difference in helping me visualize what was happening in the text. Let's begin by answering where exactly Angela Adams made the wrong tactical move in her game against Miss Dove. Angela went wrong the second she pushed her luck and added yet another sarcastic statement after she asked Miss Dove a question about the reading with the wrong intentions. _"Did he eat an ant to see? Or did a bear tell him?"_ That move was seriously wrong because Angela was way ahead of herself. She tooted her own horn before reaching the finish line. She didn't even allow Miss Dove to answer her demanded question. Which I'm sure is the reason why Angela jumps the gun and adds another sarcastic remark. She thinks she's won the game. Angela could have simply asked Miss Dove the question regarding how the author knew that the red ants tasted like pickles.

GOOD MORNING, MISS DOVE

Working with your course partner, create and submit to Mr. Eidelberg a list of all of the qualities, characteristics, values, and behaviors the two of you have traditionally associated with the kind of teacher historically known as "a schoolmarm."

Next, on YouTube, watch the first eleven minutes of the 1955 Hollywood film "Good Morning, Miss Dove," which is based on the 1954 novel of the same name by Frances Gray Patton.

Then, discuss with your partner either by email or phone, which recognizable aspects of being a schoolmarm Miss Dove exhibited in those first eleven minutes of the film, particularly those that were on your jointly submitted list. Finally, discuss with each other which schoolmarm characteristics you found to be evident in Miss Dove that were not on your list but you agree should now become part of an even more comprehensive list you will create.

Individually, each partner should submit both to Mr. Eidelberg and to the other partner, their favorite moment or moments in the film that showed Miss Dove to be a schoolmarm "par excellence."

Extra credit #1: Explain in writing to Mr. Eidelberg how the term "schoolmarm" probably came about etymologically to characterize this particular kind of public school teacher. Or, create a "folk etymology" for your explanation.

Extra credit #2: In what ways, if any, is the American teacher Miss Dove the female version of a British and schoolmarmsh Mr. Chips?

Extra credit #3: Comment on the fact that both the novel THE BLACKBOARD JUNGLE and the novel GOOD MORNING, MISS DOVE were published in the same year (1954) and that Hollywood films of these two very different (yes?) school novels were rushed into production and released to the American public the following year (1955).

Here are **course partners Shelly Uzagir and Lisa Baez** on how to recognize a schoolmarm:

- A schoolmarm may be dressed in conservative, monochromatic attire.
- A schoolmarm may be concurrently insightful, brisk and monotone.
- A schoolmarm may be punctual and consistent.
- A schoolmarm may be a no-nonsense teacher that required manners and respect in her classroom.
- A schoolmarm may be a stickler for discipline when/if her classroom rules have been broken.
- A schoolmarm may be a well-organized person.
- A schoolmarm may be a teacher who does not like to show weakness.
- A schoolmarm may be someone with great posture.
- A schoolmarm may be old-fashioned.

- A schoolmarm may have an ironic way of speaking.
- A schoolmarm may be someone who thinks they are always right.

Here are **course partners Hudaiba Khatri and Rifath Islam** on how to recognize a schoolmarm:

- Someone who is particular about her lifestyle and the manner she conducts herself in.
- She prefers a clean and proper style in terms of lifestyle and style of clothing.
- Her attitude seems a bit judgmental.
- The manner in which everyone approaches her and stares at her as she passes by the window, noting the time, suggests that she is incredibly punctual and prefers routines.
- Her style and color of clothing suggests that she is an ideal strong woman.
- Her vernacular also creates the personality that she is uninterested in anything foolish, and almost stuck up.
- Someone who has a very authoritative aura to them.
- As described in STAYING AFTER SCHOOL, Miss Dove had a reputation for trying to achieve infallibility, so they can be seen as someone who is extremely knowledgeable, giving them almost a "know-it-all" personality.
- She is refined in tastes and mannerisms.
- She seems very delicate in the way she holds herself, but has a stern exterior.

Here is how Hunter College student Danny Jiang infers the characteristics and values of "a schoolmarm" from the appearance and behavior of the teacher Miss Dove in the opening scenes (the first eleven minutes) of the 1955 feature film "Good Morning, Miss Dove":

1. The term is a variation of "madam" so a female teacher.

2. The word "infallibility" is mentioned twice in STAYING AFTER SCHOOL in the excerpt from the Patton novel. Infallibility means one who is incapable of making mistakes or being wrong, so that's an indication that a schoolmarm is a strict teacher and probably doesn't like her judgment being questioned by students.

3. Within the first five minutes of the movie, two people refer to Miss Dove as terrible, in a way indicating they may as well be sarcastically saying "the big bad Miss Dove," so a schoolmarm probably has a reputation as being a tough-to-please teacher.

4. Miss Dove dresses in all gray, and very conservatively compared to the other adult women we see in the film. Long sleeves, a high collar, a fancy hat, white gloves, and a long skirt. A schoolmarm's style is very prim and proper.

5. The first thing the audience sees Miss Dove do is oil the gate hinges on her way to work. While it is annoying to have a squeaky gate, it seems like something that could have waited until after work. So, a schoolmarm is probably a perfectionist.

6. Miss Dove proceeds to give unsolicited advice to her neighbors, indicating a schoolmarm may feel they know better than everyone else.

7. Multiple characters in the movie comment on Miss Dove's extreme punctuality, a trait I'm sure is common among shoolmarms.

8. When Miss Dove crossed the street, the traffic guard stopped all cars to make way for her. So, a schoolmarm is someone who is respected by her community – whether it be out of fear, or simply respect.

9. Miss Dove never seems to speak with much passion or emotion, every word is very carefully thought through and said almost monotonously. A schoolmarm portrays a sense of perfection and is well-composed.

10. Miss Dove's teaching style is very non-negotiable, as we see one student willingly wipe his tongue and nose with soap as a punishment with just a word from her. Miss Dove has a posture correction stool, a bell to start, pause, and resume class, and makes every student wish her a good morning before entering the room or asking any questions. A schoolmarm's teaching style is big on manners and teaching her students to give off a similar poise as herself.

11. In addition to having a non-negotiable teaching style, Miss Dove also enforces a system of rigidity. This is shown by the bell which she makes sure to ring as she announces that the class will resume their lesson following a student's interruption. Adding to this is her extreme sense of punctuality; her neighbors know what the time is based on when she passes their homes. A schoolmarm, then, is someone who values structure and order.

12. Miss Dove also has a strong sense of morality, shown by the fact that she required David to stay after class and copy the line "Nothing is achieved by swearing." However, though she punishes David, she makes sure that the assignment he must complete is able to be finished before lunch is over. Even though a schoolmarm utilized corrections to help students learn right from wrong, they are sure to not take their punishments too far.

13. Even when Miss Dove knows she is feeling very unwell, she is hesitant to ask for help, and when she finally asks David to retrieve his father, she sounds very reluctant though she speaks very clearly with well thought out instructions. Even when in an immense amount of discomfort, a schoolmarm is able to keep her composure and is very reluctant to show vulnerability or weakness, especially to students.

BONUS SESSION OF THE TEACHER AND STUDENT IN LITERATURE ON THE THIRD-GRADE PUPILS IN THE "MISS PEACH" NEWSPAPER COMIC STRIP

MISS PEACH (another "Miss"!)

Read over the next week or so any one of the paperback collections by decade of the "Miss Peach" newspaper comic strip (I particularly like the 1970's collection with little Ira and his school-provided mental health therapist).

As you experience your assortment of "Miss Peach" comic strips, keep the following question in the forefront of your mind:

What specifically American historical, societal, and cultural customs, mores, and values does this assortment represent, reflect, and reinforce (or subvert and challenge)?

Introduction to the "unremarkable" Miss Peach and her challenging class of Kelly School third-graders:

Miss Peach, of whom its creator, Mell Lazarus, said in 2008: "I didn't know a single schoolteacher who had her temperament or who was as sweet as she was. We had good teachers in the New York City school system. They really were tough. They could teach. But nobody was really sweet."

The "Miss Peach" comic strip, with its dedicated young schoolteacher and its wise-cracking Kelly School third-graders (in particular, Francine, Marcia, Ira, and Arthur) ran originally in the "The New York Herald Tribune" (a standard-format newspaper in size and shape like its then chief competitor, "The New York Times") and later (simultaneously from 1957 to 2002) in hundreds of other American newspapers across the country.

Mell Lazarus originally created the "Miss Peach" strip to enter into a talent contest sponsored by a national newspaper syndicate after he had "scanned the papers and there was nothing about school" in any of them. (He didn't win the national syndicate contest but the "Herald Tribune" in New York City picked up the strip he submitted anyway.)

Prompt #1:
Which was your favorite Ira strip – and why? Which for Francine – and why? Which for Marcia – and why? Which for Arthur – and why?

Prompt #2:
If comic strips could speak (oh, wait a minute, they do!), what do the Miss Peach comic strips tell us about 1970's America? Do they also speak (how?, how not?) to the America of today?

CW/HW CREATIVE WRITING ASSIGNMENT

Create your own multi-panel comic strip (your choice of actual or fictional characters) that makes a combined visual and verbal comment on the state of education in America today; your strip can either be drawn to the best of your stick-figure ability or you can write a verbal description of what is shown and said (in the dialogue balloons) in each of your storyboard panels.

SESSION #18 OF THE TEACHER AND STUDENT IN LITERATURE ON BRAND-NEW TEACHER URSULA BRANGWEN AND WILLIAMS, HER MOST CHALLENGING STUDENT, FROM D.H. LAWRENCE'S 1915 NOVEL THE RAINBOW

SO YOU THINK YOU MIGHT LIKE TO TEACH

Read in Chapter 6 of SO YOU THINK YOU MIGHT LIKE TO TEACH page 90 (bottom) to page 102, a fictional case study of a 17-year-old female teacher (Ursula Brangwen) from a chapter ("The Man's World") in D.H. Lawrence's 1915 novel THE RANIBOW. Not so incidentally, this Lawrence chapter went on to inspire Mr. Eidelberg to create The Teacher and Student in Literature course for Hunter College and to write SO YOU THINK YOU MIGHT LIKE TO TEACH (both based on the idea that fictional teachers can serve as mentors of sorts to prospective New York City public school teachers).

Possible Prompts (choose TWO of the three listed below and send your responses to Mr. Eidelberg and to your course partner):

(a) In the very last lines of this chapter of his book Mr. Eidelberg writes that he considers this chapter (Chapter 6 out of a total of eight chapters) to be the "saddest" in all of SO YOU THINK YOU MIGHT LIKE TO TEACH. What are your thoughts and feelings on this?

(b) Note the similarities between the fictional British teenager Ursula Brangwen and the fictional American teenager Ella Bishop from the novel MISS BISHOP (and the Hollywood movie CHEERS FOR MISS BISHOP) on page 20 of SO YOU THINK YOU MIGHT LIKE

TO TEACH. Explain why you agree or disagree that both Ursula and Ella seem to be on their way to becoming schoolmarms.

(c) What are the specific strengths and weakness of the Hunter College student persuasive essay about Ursula Brangwen that is reprinted on pages 100 – 102?

BONUS SESSION OF THE TEACHER AND STUDENT IN LITERATURE ON ROBERT COOVER'S 2016 SHORT BUT NOT SIMPLE STORY "THE HANGING OF THE SCHOOLMARM"

THE HANGING OF THE SCHOOLMARM

Read (and re-read maybe even twice more): "The Hanging of the Schoolmarm," American author Robert Coover's fairly short but quite challenging story (with its original and revealing cover illustration); first published in 2016 in THE NEW YORKER magazine and available free online (search "The Hanging of the Schoolmarm")

Prompt *(a fairly comprehensive and extended prompt to be sent to Mr. Eidelberg and to your course partner):*

I strongly recommend, however, that you and your partner FIRST exchange rough drafts of your initial written responses to this extended prompt (or discuss your analytic thoughts together on the telephone) so that both of you can benefit from feedback that you would then incorporate into your final polished version, which gets sent to both Mr. Eidelberg and your partner:

What connotations (associations, assumptions, and implications) about "schoolmarms" did you bring to your reading of this story? Where, specifically, did the story reinforce OR subvert those connotations? Which plot events and character actions that you expected to happen happened? What happened in the story that surprised you and maybe even shocked you? And, seriously about this "funny" story: What do YOU make of the story's meanings, its ideas, its confusing moments, its attitudes, its points of view, the questions it may leave unanswered (for you) or the problems it may leave unresolved (for you)? What larger statements that the author might be making do you now think you understand, and why might it have taken a second or third reading of the story for you to come to any of these understandings?

Here is how Rifath Islam sees teachers who are schoolmarms:

The only prior knowledge of a "schoolmarm" that I brought with myself to this reading of "The Hanging of the Schoolmarm" was that which I gathered upon my completion of reading the excerpt of "Good Morning, Miss Dove." As such, this meant my assumption of how the schoolmarm would be portrayed in this story would be similar to that of Miss Dove, a prim and proper lady who was very refined and her manners were nothing short of "lady-like," while still managing to elicit obedience from her disciples. In some ways, the schoolmarm from this story both contributed and contrasted to this assumption that I brought into this reading. On the one hand, the nameless schoolmarm of this story does feed into the previous assumption I had when she is described as "not going together" with cussing (hence the men refrain from it around her) as how she instituted as teaching regimen amongst them in what was previously a saloon. Yet, on the other hand, I found this image contradicted right away in the beginning when she is said to shoot a man upon receiving a demand from him and in the way she physically disciplines the men when she finds them not giving her respect.

That being said, the demand for respect that the schoolmarm expects from the men is very much expected. Though the actions and methods she utilizes were slightly questionable, the idea in general was not shocking. However, there were many *other* shocking points throughout this short story. For example, to bring up again is the fact that the schoolmarm shoots a man upon his gruff command. As I expected a mannered, refined woman, this part caught me slightly off guard, as it seems like a very ill-controlled move, even unreasonable. Additionally, the part where all the men collectively decided to hang the schoolmarm caught me extremely off guard because despite the fact that she was incredibly rough with them, it still seemed like an extreme measure to put her to death.

This story was definitely one of the more challenging ones to understand, leaving me with many questions. For example, what is the significance of the rocks in comparison to the entirety of the story? What lesson is this story even meant to teach? After reading it over several times and searching for different ways to analyze this story, I think I have finally pieced together a semblance of understanding of what this story is trying to teach. Of all the characters in this story, the schoolmarm is the main one, and she represents knowledge and lack of fear, in the way she seemed very nonchalant at the idea of being hanged. The men, on the other hand, represent the students and lack of knowledge. The schoolmarm is attempting to transfer her knowledge to the men, though they seem impartial to it, uninterested in learning anything she has to offer. The sheriff and the men seem to have a baseline understanding of the world and its working, and this is clearly demonstrated in the way the sheriff announces himself as an expert on justice. However, he says justice is served depending on "the color of the law that was broken, and at what time of day or night order got criminally disordered." At most, this is a superficial understanding of justice, it is simply following a rulebook – the law - without truly applying any more thought to it. As the schoolmarm attempts to give a deeper explanation of what justice is, the men nod off as they do not care to learn and because what she is saying is beyond their understanding. The schoolmarm is almost seen as a higher being than the men because of her lack of fear of death and because of the seemingly endless knowledge that she has, that the others lack to comprehend. I think that another major idea that Coover perhaps was trying to embody in this story is lack of justice. The schoolmarm's work with the men helped implement a system of law, and under this system of law the men decided to put the schoolmarm to death because they dislike her methods. Not only is this a display of the irony that the schoolmarm spoke of in her last moments, but it demonstrates the lack of justice is an embodiment of the fears in the sheriff and his men of a higher level of understanding.

Here is how Victoria Cecere sees teachers who are schoolmarms:

There were many connotations of the "schoolmarm" that I brought with me when reading "The Hanging of the Schoolmarm." The first is the inability to tolerate disrespect or ill-mannered behavior. We see this at the beginning, where the schoolmarm shoots the man that screams for her to just "cut the f*ckin' deck." This trait is also re-asserted when the author states that the men like to cuss, but will never do so around the schoolmarm. This added information shows just how respected the schoolmarm is – as disrespect and ill-manners are clearly not tolerated by her. The second is her formal and professional composition. The schoolmarm is still uninterested in small talk, speaks professionally and assertively, and enacts her will on the people and things around her. We see this with the transformation of the saloon. After winning, the schoolmarm is quick to turn the saloon into a school. She creates a school where she could teach all of the local men their spelling as well as other basic subjects. Her goal was to get them to speak correctly and to give up any bad habits they have picked up. Though her punishments are harsh, they certainly get the job done in making the men learn their lessons. However, the men are unable to handle the expectations and repercussions provided by the schoolmarm. Even when she is about to be hanged, we see this schoolmarm act much like Miss Dove in her ability to keep students learning. Even when things begin to get rough, she continues to provide a lesson for her students. For Miss Dove, she taught through illness. Through this schoolmarm, she taught through the events leading up to her execution.

However, this schoolmarm's added monologue before her death did surprise me. I did not expect the schoolmarm to break away from the traditional connotation as one who did not appreciate talk that felt meaningless. For the others surrounding the schoolmarm, the monologue seemed useless, especially considering they could not understand it. Through that time, she still managed to hide any weaknesses or fear she may have had because of her need to keep her image. Although she would die, she seemed to want to leave a lasting impact on the students she had. The schoolmarm was and always would be considered something ineffable. She was someone that was unchanging.

The story did answer many of my questions regarding other schoolmarms. However, I still wanted to know what she felt about being betrayed by her students. In my eyes, she had simply been doing her job. Although I don't believe in beating students, the schoolmarm has a goal in mind and strived to complete it as best as possible. I wanted to know if she felt pained or sad. Though she would have hidden it regardless, it confused me that she did not address her feelings about being forced to death herself, as this would be the last time she would be able to do so. Regardless of that, I didn't find the story as "funny" as I think others might have. Instead, I think I focused too hard on the schoolmarm that I was trying to figure out. Almost like a puzzle. I wanted to know what went through her head about the situation after she had done so much (including shooting a man) to create a school of her own.

BONUS SESSION OF THE TEACHER AND STUDENT IN LITERATURE ON TEACHING SOME ONE SOME THING (OR SOMETHING, ANYTHING) INSPIRED BY E. L. KONIGSBURG'S 1966 YOUNG ADULT NOVEL THE VIEW FROM SATURDAY

STAYING AFTER SCHOOL

Read all of Chapter 7 in the text STAYING AFFTER SCHOOL to learn how to teach in other than a full classroom setting (perhaps in the spirit and style of Theophilus North's private tutorials, as mentioned in the opening chapter to Mr. Eidelberg's other text SO YOU THINK YOU MIGHT LIKE TO TEACH).

Prompt #1:
Of the five how-to tutorials written by former Hunter College students, which is your favorite – and why?

Prompt #2:
With respect to "Instructions on How to Belch on Command – and Other Teaching Moments" (the excerpt from E.L Konigsburg's 1966 young adult novel THE VIEW FROM SATURDAY), how does Mrs. Olinski's methodology with her sixth-graders illustrate the truth of the following maxim about teaching and learning: *"Teach me, I forget; show me, I remember; involve me, I understand"*? If you can, also relate an educational experience you have had that confirmed the truth of this maxim for you.

CW/HW
Create a private tutorial of your own that describes, explains, and teaches something (or "some thing") to your course partner. Choose something – a behavior, an activity, or a skill – that you really like being knowledgeable about and modestly think yourself really quite good at doing.

Get on-going revision feedback from your course partner as you try out your "how-to" lesson plan on them and come to understand how their lack of skill may be the result of unclear or missing steps in your rough draft tutorial.

After submitting a final version of your "how-to" tutorial to Mr. Eidelberg, discuss with your course partner the relative truth for each of you of the following statement: teaching someone else how to do something you believed you were close to an expert at actually taught you something about the process that you only inexactly understood.

Here is Hunter College student Martin Ljuljduraj's tutorial on "How to master the art of being a doorman":

Being a doorman sounds like it's an easy gig; this is exactly what I thought until I went to go train for five days with two different full-time doormen. He taught me every little thing that I have to remember to do. I have been working as a part-time doorman in Manhattan for a few months now and it hasn't been a struggle for me, but then again I was in training with the right people and because of that I know what to do in every situation. At first, however, there were many situations that happened during my training that I had no clue were things that I must look out for. Now, I am confident in saying that I have "mastered" the job of being a doorman and I will go over what one must do in order to master this art.

Stay on your feet: as stated, you must literally remain standing for most of the duration of the whole shift, which is eight hours, I say "most" because there are a couple times where one may rest on the stool provided for a small period of time. I work from 3 pm to 11 pm on Sundays and so there are a good number of tenants walking in and out of the building and you must obviously open the door every time.

Security: you will be at the door pretty much at all times since you are in a way a security guard. In addition to that, there are cameras that you have right next door for anyone coming in or leaving. It is your job to recognize the tenants who live in the building so that you do not let people that you do not recognize inside. If there is an unauthorized person in the building and you do not go to stop them and ask who they are, a tenant can complain to management and you will be liable. There are also the possibilities that you may get suspended or even fired as a result.

Giving packages to tenants: There are packages and groceries that come in virtually everyday from the morning until late in the afternoon and it is your job to take them in from the steps outside the door and bring them in. This is a protocol especially due to the virus and social distancing requirements. For the groceries, it is important that you read the labels to see what apartment they are for, then call the tenant immediately as for the most part they are perishable items. For packages, you must check all items and see what apartment they are for, where they came from (Fedex, UPS, Lasership, etc.) and then you mark all of the boxes with the apartment number and put them all in the BuildingLink system on the computer which is at your desk. Whenever you see a tenant coming in that has a package, tell them how many packages they have and give them to the tenant.

Smile and keep a good posture: posture is important because if you are slouching, having your hands in your pockets, or for whatever reason sleeping, tenants will inform management and you will get in trouble (serious trouble if you are "sleeping"). It also gives the tenants a sense of security when they see you are standing straight and will not have to worry about you not doing your job. Also, it doesn't hurt to cut a smile as you want to show the tenants that you are attentive and overall someone that they would like to continue having around. Tenants want this kind of doorman as it gives them the impression that you are attentive and awake at every moment, which also helps you avoid being confronted by your supervisor. When everyone there isn't worried, you aren't worried.

Here is Hunter College student Victoria Cecere's meta-tutorial on how to write a how-to tutorial:

This is something that not many people recognize how to do. Many people feel like they can create how-to's, but get lost during the process. Luckily, I've created a how-to about how to write a how-to. Try to say that three times fast!

Step One, you need to pick a topic. Don't worry, this does not have to be your final topic. Instead, it should be something that you feel you can write enough about. If you get struck, don't worry! There are so many other options you can choose from. The sky is the limit! If you find yourself unable to pick a preliminary topic – ask a friend or family member for help! They may suggest things like recipes, or even how to tie your shoes. If you feel like you do not have enough information you can continue to Step Two.

Step Two, you need to do some research. Even if you feel like you have a "good-enough" idea of what your topic is all about and how to describe the how-to for said topic, it may not be enough. Doing research ensures that you have a large amount of information to choose from. As you continue writing, you will omit unnecessary information and include vital information. This is obviously subjective, and may not be the same for everyone. But, having a large amount of information to pick from gives you your own security blanket to lean on. As you continue to research, you may need to adjust your topic accordingly. If so, no sweat! You can go back to the earlier steps and repeat until you have a topic with enough research to support your ideas. From there, you can continue to Step Three.

Step Three, it's time to start writing! Don't worry, you will be proofreading and making edits in the next few steps. During this step, however, you should try to get all of your ideas and vital pieces of information onto paper. Having your research organized will help you a lot with this step. More organization makes this easier to write and understand, so keep things neat! Usually, I try to give myself an allotted amount of time, and only write during that time. After writing for that specific amount of time, I will go back and see what I have created. If it does not make sense, I may need to start again with more time. That, or I may need to adjust my topic again. The goal here is to get down important ideas, but without taking up too much time. There is still a bit left to be done, so this is the time to make your information really count. After you have completed your initial writing, and are satisfied with what you have created, it is time to move on to Step Four.

Step Four, time to proofread. This step is a bit time-consuming, but it is one of the most important steps. You should pay close attention to structure and organization as you make corrections. The how-to should be in some kind of order, though most follow a chronological order in order to make sense. However, not all topics need to use that same order, as some tutorials do not follow typical guidelines. For the ones that do not need chronological order, there should still be some understanding of what order things should be done in. This is the place to turn your writing into something magnificent! If you need, you are more than welcome to go back and write another version of the preliminary writing and compare the two. That may help, as you can take vital pieces from both creations and merge them together into something you are proud of. Keep proofreading and editing until you are happy with your results, then it is finally time to continue to Step Five.

Step Five, time for the finale! Here, you should have a piece of writing that you are ready to submit or publish. Remember, this piece may be seen by those outside of the intended audience. With that in mind, make sure that what you wrote is something you would be comfortable sharing with others. You should be able to recite your "recipe" for success at this point. After that, the rest is dependent on where you are submitting this piece. You may need to send this document as an attachment to a professor, or as an email to a publishing company. Either way, make sure you know what you have to send, as well as *when* you have to send it. Your how-to should be sent in on time and should be legible by others. I suggest that you type your how-to out it possible, with Times New Roman, in twelve-point font. After getting to the specified submission area, you should make certain that you have your preferred name on the piece, as well as a title! The title does not have to be anything special, but should definitely relate to your piece's main ideas; this is necessary only if you have not done so already, because most writers title their pieces during the preliminary writing stages. Now that you have your beautiful piece, placed in the proper area for submission, you are ready to submit and be done with said assignment.

Congratulations, you've finished!

SESSION #19 OF THE TEACHER AND STUDENT IN LITERATURE ON THE 1937 STAR-STUDDED NOVEL THE EDUCATION OF H*Y*M*A*N K*A*P*L*A*N

⎰

(an urban depression-era novel by Leo Rosten; the original penname on the novel was Leonard Q. Ross; Leo Rosten is also famous for his 534-page 1968 non-fiction work THE JOYS OF YIDDISH)

The title of our next novel in The Teacher and Student in Literature suggests an emphasis on "the Student" more than on "the Teacher" since it begins with the words "the education of." Of course, as I believe we have discovered in this course, you can't have one without the other (like the two sides of a coin), so I think you will agree (after you've read the novel straight through) that Mr. Kaplan's teacher – the pedantic but concerned and frustrated Mr. Parkhill at the American Night Preparatory School for Adults – definitely learns a thing or two about teaching and learning from his star-student but "problem case," the one-of-a-kind Mr. Kaplan.

I don't think you will find THE EDUCATION OF HYMAN KAPLAN (note: I only do the stars on the first mention of the title!) to be too dated or too non-universally ethnic or too Yiddish-y corny (too Great Depression 1930's, too stereotypically immigrant Jewish, too linguistically demanding and too broad in its comic appeal). Anyway, I hope not.

And here, for now, are some think-about-only (no writing about yet!) questions that might work to focus your reading:

- *How is Hyman Kaplan a sort of "teacher's pet" for Mr. Parkhill – and how do the other students in the class feel about that?*

- *Do you agree or disagree (and why, specifically) with those literary critics who consider this short American novel to be not only a "hilarious, timeless tale" but also THE classic ode (tribute) to the urban American immigrant experience in and with education?*

Some further background: The novel consists of fifteen linked stories (fictional "case studies") set in New York City during the worldwide Great Depression of the 1930's and, what may be unique in school literature, not just a few but all of its narrative scenes take place in a classroom. More particularly, it is an evening school classroom for some thirty-odd adults (mostly male and female Jewish immigrants, but other ethnic and religious groups as well) who are trying to improve their English language skills (they mostly speak Yiddish, which is linguistically close to German, or they speak English with a heavy Yiddish pronunciation and accent).

These students' goal? To pass the naturalization test to become American citizens – that's their "American dream" (one still very much in the news today in a country that is historically "a nation of immigrants"). The official name of the class says it all: "English–Americanization–Civics–Preparation for Naturalization." (Have you or members of your extended family had similar or comparable experiences in any kind of school?)

As the novel opens, Mr. Kaplan's teacher – the very WASP (White Anglo-Saxon Protestant) Mr. Parkhill – is musing (somewhat like Rick Dadier did in THE BLACKBOARD JUNGLE) over whether he might have a problem recommending Mr. Kaplan for promotion to the next grade (and to a different teacher) when the current school year is up. And who is this Mr. Kaplan who, in a weird but explainable way, is "teacher's pet"? Hyman Kaplan is a man in his forties who works full-time during the day (this is night school, remember) as a garment "cotter" (Mr. Kaplan's variable-voweled version and Yiddish-inflected pronunciation for a "cutter" (of cloth), that is to say, a "pattern-maker" in a dress factory).

Here are three *different kinds* of "amazing renditions of the English language" (early in the novel from the mind and experience of its author Leo Rosten, out of the mouth of his most famous creation, Hyman Kaplan):

- on page 19: Mr. Kaplan answers that the opposite of "new" is **"second-hand"** instead of "old" (because of his clothing background in the garment industry);

- on page 45: "verbal indiscretions" were caused, according to Mr. Kaplan, by a **"sleeping of the tong"**; had he pronounced his vowels correctly and knew English grammar better, Mr. Kaplan would have said, instead, something closer to "a slip of the tongue";
- on page 3: Mr. Kaplan gives the plural of "cat" as "Katz" (a familiar Jewish surname (last name) spelled that way in writing and too often stereotypically mispronounced as "ketts"); the correct plural is "cats."

Prompts to think about as you read Leo Rosten's THE EDUCATION OF HYMAN KAPLAN over the next few sessions:

When you are about three quarters of the way through the novel, choose and write about two of the following prompts and submit both to Mr. Eidelberg and your course partner along with the "in-voice" creative writing assignment that follows the five prompt choices.

1. How is the teacher in this novel, Mr. Parkhill, similar to and yet different from the other fictional teachers we have read about so far this semester?

2. How are the various adult students of this novel similar to and yet different from the adolescent students we have read about to this point in the semester?

3. How is the "classroom life" of the American Night Preparatory School for Adults different from and yet similar to the literary classrooms we have "attended" so far in this course?

4. How is this very American novel a universal ode (tribute) to teachers and students (as well as to live non-remote teaching and learning)? How does this question resonate with you and for you personally in the United States today?

5. How is this novel a twentieth-century ode (tribute) to America as a "nation of immigrants"? How does this question resonate with you and for you personally in the United States today?

Required "in-voice" CW/HW as you read Leo Rosten's *THE EDUCATION OF HYMAN KAPLAN* over the next few sessions:

Pretend you are one of Mr. Kaplan's fellow classmates in the immigration-focused adult night school and in that person's voice write a letter of complaint to Mr. Parkhill about his treatment of you as compared with his treatments of Mr. Kaplan. The content and sound of your personal letter should be enough as to reveal who you are, but just in case, be sure to sign your Dr. Mr. Parkhill letter with your fictional character's name.

SESSION #20 OF THE TEACHER AND STUDENT IN LITERATURE ON THE CLASSROOM IN LEO ROSTEN'S THE EDUCATION OF H*Y*M*A*N K*A*P*L*A*N

Your reading and thinking assignment:
Read the novel straight through over the next week, paying primary attention, in this character-driven work, to Hyman Kaplan's relationship with his fellow students, with his teacher, and, of course, with himself. Please do NOT worry about understanding every single piece of wit and wisdom that comes out of Hyman Kaplan's mouth (not possible for us today); there's plenty (enough) that you WILL figure out once you get into the swing of things – and there's more than enough to smile at (maybe even laugh at loud at). If you want to email me about being crazy bothered by a particularly puzzling punchline, feel free; however, caveat emptor (buyer beware): there is nothing in language study that falls flatter than a joke whose punchline needs to be explained.

A recommendation: read the first chapter or so either out loud to yourself or aloud to a family member or friend: doing this will help you to both "get" and "get with" the sound, the feel, and the "hang" of the weirdly logical reasoning engaged in by the unique character at this novel's center, who even had his school story made – would you believe? – into a Broadway musical that was so unsuccessful (such a flop!) that it got no stars. Finally, I hope you will come to know this lover of learning and veritable "star" of his own life as he undergoes his dreamed-of "education" because H*Y*M*A*N K*A*P*L*A*N:

- is high-spirited, irrepressible, indomitable – an earnest and enthusiastic "Student" with a capital "S" who signs all his written work with a nine "star-studded" signature in red, blue, and green;

- has only one desire and that is to be the center of attention and impress his teacher, Mr. Parkhill (who "clung with undaunted faith" to the method of "direct participation" and sometimes wondered whether Mr. Kaplan "might not be some sort of genius");
- has a strong sense of himself in competition with the other students in the class, particularly "no such woid" Mr. Norman Bloom, and "oi!" "poor Mrs. Moskowitz who simply had no ear for sounds," and the shy Miss Rose Mitnik, who was "easily the best student in the class";
- has an ongoing problem of applying his German-sounding Yiddish pronunciation patterns to American English vocabulary, grammar, spelling, idioms, you name it (and say it loud and correctly!).

Required prompt to be sent to both Mr. Eidelberg and your course partner upon completion of the novel:

How did you wind up decoding student Hyman Kaplan's idiosyncratic language choices so that you were able to get the serious points author Leo Rosten was making through his humorous word play?

Required CW/HW (choose one of the following) to be sent to both Mr. Eidelberg and your couse partner upon completion of the novel:

1. Write a letter from Hyman Kaplan to his teacher Mr. Parkhill explaining exactly and specifically why (reflecting the closing words of the novel) you "love the class" and don't care that you may not be promoted out of it to the next grade and another teacher (although you are under *no obligation* to sound like Mr. Kaplan – and you certainly know what that means – in his letter to the pedantic Mr. Parkhill, *feel free to go for it* in his voice (vocabulary, pronunciation, and grammar) if you like a challenge (and some extra credit);

OR

2. Write a letter from Mr. Parkhill – and *definitely* in his pedantic WASP voice (and vocabulary and grammar) – to Hyman Kaplan telling Mr. Kaplan exactly how he has been his most "challenging" student *ever* and yet did *not deserve* to be promoted to the next grade and another teacher (and how he feels about continuing as Mr. Kaplan's teacher).

OPTIONAL (EXTRA CREDIT) ASSIGNMENT: WORLD OF OUR FATHERS

In connection with our study of the novel THE EDUCATION OF HYMAN KAPLAN, **read** in Irving Howe's WORLD OF OUR FATHERS the chapters on Jewish immigration to the United States that deal specifically with their education in New York City; then turn in an extra credit **personal essay** on the following question: How was *your* experience (or the experience of members of your extended family or of friends of yours or of your family) with public education in the United States similar to or different from that of these Jewish immigrants?

OPTIONAL (EXTRA CREDIT) ASSIGNMENT: HARD TIMES

Read the case study on pages 86 - 90 in SO YOU THINK YOU MIGHT LIKE TO TEACH of model school superintendent and teacher Thomas Gradgrind; then turn in an extra credit **personal essay** on the following question: Given the "hard times" for students inside "the culture" of this "model" school, speculate on what the "hard times" are like in the general culture of its 19th-century industrial society of Coketown. How are the "hard times" of THE EDUCATION OF HYMAN KAPLAN (it's set in the Great Depression of 1930's America, after all) similar or not similar to the "hard times" of HARD TIMES (it's set, as I said above, in 19th-century industrial revolution Britain)? And how is the satire of the author Leo Rosten similar or not similar to the satire of the author Charles Dickens?

OPTIONAL (EXTRA CREDIT) CW/HW on Language Play (Acronym-Making) due to Mr. Eidelberg and you course partner by the completion of our study of THE EDUCATION OF HYMAN KAPLAN

Read Chapter 9 in STAYING AFTER SCHOOL, an insightful and imaginative (the ideal combination!) Hunter College student-written chapter on "What-if Words of Education Wisdom" (pages 96-99); the entire chapter consists of many of the course's words that came up in an earlier class of The Teacher and Student in Literature; all of these words that soon became acronyms for the class were created very quickly in the final moments of the semester – that's why they were given their own meaningful acronym term "HURRY" (which stood for, we decided, letter by letter just the way acronyms are meant to do: "Haste Under Rapidly Receding Year").

After you read this quite short but pretty comprehensive chapter in STAYING AFTER SCHOOL, I thought it would be highly appropriate while we are studying a novel about language that we all think about the particular words that come to mind when we look back on our reading of and writing about Leo Rosten's THE EDUCATION OF HYMAN KAPLAN and then choose one (or more, if you like) that could be a meaningful acronym (once you ran it by and explained it to your course partner).

For example, my acronym "HYMAN," to be tested with my course partners (that's all of you!), would be our major character's first name – Hyman – standing meaningfully, I hope and think, for the core essence of this particular man's personality. The acronym "HYMAN" represents, letter by letter, "How You Manage a Nudnik."

For what a "nudnik" is, see below the excerpt from Leo Rosten's other famous book THE JOYS OF YIDDISH.

> nudnik
>
> Pronounced NUD-*nick,* to rhyme with "could pick." *Nudnik* may come form the Russian *nudna,* but it has become as uniquely Yiddish a word as there is. It is sometimes pronounces NUD-*nyik,* just as *paskudnak* is often pronounced *poss-kood-NYUK,* by those who wish to add a vocal prolongation of distaste.
>
> A *nudnik* is not just a nuisance; to merit the status of *nudnik,* a nuisance must be a most persistent, talkative, obnoxious, indomitable, and indefatigable nag. I regard *nudnik* as a peerless word for the characterization of a universal type.
>
> A mother often says to a child, "Stop bothering me. Don't be a *nudnik!*"
>
> Morris Rosenfeld, the poet, wrote an entire essay on the *nudnik,* whom he defines as a man "whose purpose in life is to bore the rest of humanity."

Mr. Polanski complained to his doctor, "Something terrible has happened to me. I try to stop it, but I can't.... Morning, noon, and night – I keep talking to myself!"

"Now, now," the doctor crooned, "that isn't such a bad habit. Why, thousands of people do it."

"But, doctor," protested Polanski, "you don't know what a *nudnik* I am!"

Here is how Rifath Islam responded to the prompt about the nature of classroom life in THE EDUCATION OF HYMAN KAPLAN and to the "in-voice" assignment of writing as student Norman Bloom a letter of protest about a teacher's playing favorites among his students.

The most common trend that was seen among many of the classrooms that have been "attended" throughout this course is that of misbehavior. Among the first two to three classrooms that were explored in the beginning of this course, many of the students were seen as "juvenile delinquents" completely uninterested in learning and doing their best work to divert their teacher from their course of schoolwork. However, in THE EDUCATION OF HYMAN KAPLAN, many of the students seem incredibly engaged with their work, even eager to complete the many assignments that Mr. Parkhill assigns them. They are what can be defined as "go-getters," contrary to the students in Dadier and Sir's class initially, when they seemed like the last thing they wanted in the world was to learn. However, the students in Dadier and Sir's class, much like the students in Mr. Parkhill's class, all worship their teachers (at least towards the end) because all these teachers seem to have a remarkable effect on the students in that they are aiding them in achieving a large goal, whether it be moving on as adults or learning English. Additionally, in many of the initial classrooms that were visited earlier on in this course, many of the students stood in solidarity with each other, as it was a situation with the students teaming up against the teacher, but in this story, it seems more like Hyman Kaplan vs. Mr. Parkhill. Overall, there seems to be a more upbeat aura in Mr. Parkhill's class than in any other.

Dear Teacher Mr. Parkhill,

When I joined your class I very much enjoy it. You are very good teacher and helped me with my English alot. But I do not like this Mr. Kaplan in our class. He is making lot of troble and often make too many mistakes.

When we do class work on the Blackboard he talk too much and is often rude when we tell him of mistakes. He is often rude to me as well when I tell him of his mistakes with his work. But you do not tell him he is being rude to me and the students. I think you shud tell Mr. Kaplan that his work is no good and he have to learn better because he does not do his work very good. He is a fun student but I think that he need to be better in class and you need to tell him. But I think you are very good teacher and I like your class alot.

Regards,

Norman Bloom

Required CW/HW Prompt: Pretend that you are one of Hyman Kaplan's fellow classmates in the immigrant-focused adult high school - and in that person's voice write a letter of complaint to Mr. Parkhill about his treatment of you as compared with his treatment of Hyman Kaplan. The content and sound of your personal letter should be enough to reveal who you are, but just in case, be sure to sign your Dear Teacher Mr. Parkhill letter with your fictional character's name.

Dear Mr. Parkhill,

Please do not take this the wrong way, because you have taught me so much, but I have to get this off my chest. I find myself leaving class every evening upset - upset at the fact that I am *treated so differently. I do not want to put words in my classmates' mouths, but I can assure you* that most of them probably feel the same way. If Hyman is your favorite, then just flat out say it but it is unfair that we are left feeling this way. Why does he get more time than me? Why do you seem to care about his progress more than mine? For the majority of every single class, the spotlight is always on Mr. Kaplan and I cannot take it anymore. Why do you allow him to take up so much for our *shared* class time? If one of us gets something wrong, it's just flat out wrong. There is no praise for trying, no working through the question with your help, no second chances - we are just flat out wrong. But when Hyman gets a question wrong you will sit there and dwell on it for the longest time. Hyman gets a question wrong: *"Not exactly, Hyman. Let's try again."* Seriously, it is unfair. It is like your patience is eternal for this man.

Hyman is irresponsible. He jokes around all class and takes every opportunity upon himself to correct someone (he's usually always wrong) and you do absolutely nothing about it. I understand that you are trying to help us with our English and all of us did not learn at the same pace, but it is getting out of hand. Hyman is a distraction. It is not fair to us to have our precious class time to be taken over by one sole person. Who is the teacher here? You or Hyman? It is time to get a grip and move the class along whenever we are losing our momentum. I admire his work ethic and his hunger for learning, and I feel bad that he is simply just not getting it, but is it worth holding back an entire class of most thirsty other students just for one student?

Please, Mr. Parkhill. Let's find a solution as a collective. Is there any way that you could meet with him for some individual extra help time before or after school? Heck, I would even have studying sessions with him even though he seems to have it out for me as he finds the need to challenge me every single class. But, that aside, just as the rest of us, he is entitled to his learning and I am sure he is just as eager for his citizenship as the rest of us are. However, the way we are going about this is harmful to the majority. Although I am sure it is not your intention, there is a clear difference in the way that Mr. Kaplan is treated than the rest of us and it makes us feel inferior. I, and hopefully you are too, am ready to fix this dilemma. I am sure the rest of the class agrees. It is my hope that this letter finds you well and you are not offended by what I have said. I just wanted to be honest with you and tell you how your other students are feeling. Regardless, your effort to help us gain access to our citizenship will never go unappreciated.

Respectfully,

Miss Mitnick.

The following pieces of correspondence between teacher Mr. Parkhill and student Hyman Kaplan are by Hunter College students Rifah Islam, Victoria Cecere, and Janel Fernandez

Dear Mr. Kaplan,

I must start off by saying that even though I am keeping you back from advancing to the next class, having you in my nightly periods was quite a pleasure. Though I must say that you must not take it personal that you have not been promoted on to Miss Higby's class, your work has presented a lens for me to see into the minds of my pupils.

Throughout the entirely of our classes, you remained one of the most enthusiastic students I have yet had, even when you could not grasp certain concepts, but you did not let it ruin your spirits. I hope you understand my decision because I feel it would be best for you to remain in my class where I can continue to work with you around the issues you encounter in learning. Having you in my class this year has been a pleasure and you have helped me to see all the different ways that people can understand and learn English. Although the next year will not be easy, I expect it to be very interesting and I am hoping that by the end of next year, I will be able to promote you to Miss Higby's class. In the meantime, I am looking forward to once again having you in my class and I hope that we can both continue learning together.

Sincerely,

Mr. Parkhill
(As voiced and written by Rifath Islam)

Dear Mr. Hyman Kaplan,

By now I am sure you know that you will not be continuing on to the next grade. Though judging by our last conversation, I now know that it does not faze you. However, I did want you to know why you will not be continuing. That may help you, as I do want you to continue learning English for your own sake. I've noticed that you make repeated mistakes, many of which we have gone over several times. You definitely need to work on your spelling and vocabulary, as both things can be improved on before you enter the classroom again next "semester." In addition, your classroom etiquette is not exactly what I'm looking for. However, I must say I do appreciate some of the jokes you make during class. But, you must learn to criticize constructively, meaning without embarrassing others in the class, as it does not make them feel very good about what they have done. The goal is to make sure that everyone learns in a safe and comfortable environment. So I would like to work with you on ways to give and take criticism - in ways that are more beneficial to you and the rest of the class. Though you do have many things to learn, I think you have the ability to improve quite drastically. I have high hopes for you this time around. As much as I appreciate your presence in my classroom, you will eventually need to graduate on to higher levels, as I won't be able to teach you in the same way that I teach the other students.

Getting back to the topic at hand, I feel that having you in my classroom again will actually be very beneficial to you. There will be more time to learn and expand your knowledge of the language and necessary etiquette needed to do well for yourself and make your family very proud. I hope that one day you and your brother will be able to see each other again, hopefully in your new home in America! I would like to encourage you to write letters to your family once a week. I will look over them personally after class, as I think this may help you work out some of the errors we would like to move on from. From there, I can definitely help you send them out to your family members if you would like. Either way, we have a lot of work to do! We also have a lot of progress to make!

I look forward to seeing you in class next semester.

All the best,

Mr. Parkhill
(As voiced and written by Victoria Cecere)

Dear Mr. Pockheel,

I just vant to say that I love your teachink and I have done lost of improvking. Soch a fine titcher ve all got. You are such a netcheral. I tell you dis all da time. But love to tell you again. Before I know noting about inglish and now I know lost of tinks know about Julius Scissor and Shaksbeer. I love when we has opinkweschons, vocapulary is also instrstink. You also inchroducink me to poetry. I love poetry. I vrote you sometink please teke look:

I happi dat you are my titcher.
I love eich lesson you titch.
It is because of you all my gols are reeched
You are pachent, you are kind
You are my numer one
All da time
YAAAAYA! (dat is menink excitement) Mr. Pockheel

I hope you like my poetry. I am no shaksbeer, but he inspire (dishonary say it menink to fill wit pashon) me to writink this poyem. See Mr. Pockheel. I dont care If I dont pass love the class.

Affectionately,
H*Y*M*A*N K*A*P*L*A*N
(As voiced and written by Janel Fernandez)

SESSION #21 OF THE TEACHER AND STUDENT IN LITERATURE ON MURIEL SPARK'S 1962 NOVEL THE PRIME OF MISS JEAN BRODIE

THE PRIME OF MISS JEAN BRODIE

We are about to meet another adult female teacher (another schoolmarm?, well you decide) in the prime, she says, of her life – her teaching life and her personal life (you decide whether the two can be separated). This fictional teacher is the famous (infamous?) creation of the Scottish author Muriel Spark (who died in 2006 at the age of 86) and her name is Miss Jean Brodie. Spark's 1962 novel was made into a play by Jay Presson Allen that your instructor saw on Broadway in 1968 (yes!). It starred the renowned Australian actress Zoe Caldwell as the imperious Jean Brodie in a performance that deservedly won Miss Caldwell the prestigious Tony award that year for best actress in a play.

Miss Allen later adapted her play for the screen with the phenomenal British actress Maggie Smith in an Oscar award-winning best actress role as Jean Brodie; your instructor advises you to NOT see the film until you have read Spark's short novel. Why? Because if you see the film first you will not be able to get Smith's performance out of your head, eyes, and ears, and so it will be virtually impossible for you to visualize and hear a Jean Brodie of your own from interactions with Muriel Spark's notable prose. (Of all the works of literature studied in this course, this novel is the only one that is commonly taught in American secondary schools and colleges as part of the common core canon.)

There is also in the feature film a romantic theme song called "Jean" that could wind up being an earworm for you for the rest of your life but is (and note that the song is called "Jean" and not "Miss Jean Brodie," a distortion of the portrait that Muriel Spark paints of her title character with precise language choices and the structured use of the technique known as "time shift" (currently made important use of in the network television series "This Is Us").

Read: Chapters 1, 2, and 3 of this short novel

Prompts (your responses to two out of the following three prompts are to be emailed to both Mr. Eidelberg and your course partner):

#1: I have mentioned in connection with our study of THE BLACKBOARD JUNGLE that how an author begins a work of fiction is worth taking notice of and thinking about. So, whom does author Muriel Spark make us meet on the first six pages of the novel and how are these characters presented to us (in what sequence and in what manner)? Did you expect to meet the title character first and right away?

#2: What are your very first impressions of these students and teachers – and what do you base them on? Where do your impressions get confirmed or rethought in the rest of Chapter 1 and all of Chapters 2 and 3? What surprises you about how the characters and the plot begin to play out?

#3: If you were making a movie of this novel, how would the start of your movie be similar to (in terms of images and sounds) or different from what Muriel Spark makes you see and hear in her first two chapters?

For further focusing of your reading during your study of this novel, check out the questions for general readers and book club participants at the very end of your edition: "Discussion Topics," pages 15 and 16.

Also, you might want to check out online the major beliefs of the Protestant sect known as Calvinism (named after John Calvin). Calvinism's interpretation of the generally Protestant idea of "predestination" is predestination with a twist, since strict Calvinists live out their earthly lives believing that a Christian God has determined each person's earthly course and after life fate BEFORE you are born and not only can you not know what God has authoritatively decided but there is nothing you (or anyone or anything) can do in this earthly life to affect or alter what is, literally, "God knows," the secret of your fate.

Please further note that Jean Brodie is a Calvinist and as we've seen in our study of other works of teacher literature this term, religious beliefs and values can and do affect public education policy. Note, too, that the other - and contrasting - religion that appears in THE PRIME OF MISS JEAN BRODIE is Roman Catholicism (which Spark herself converted to), which does not hold with predestination, at all, and one of the ways in which Muriel Spark reveals potential conflicts between Jean Brodie and a member of her set is to shift back and forth in time in order to reference either or both of these two religions.

Calvinism (and Catholicism) in THE PRIME OF MISS JEAN BRODIE

The main character in the novel (set in the late 1920's through the late 1950's) is Miss Jean Brodie, a Scottish Calvinist.

Another character in the novel is a nun (Roman Catholicism).

Two quotations from the novel:

1. "She thinks she is Providence, thought Sandy, she thinks she is the God of Calvin, she sees the beginning and the end."
2. John Calvin's doctrine of **predestination (seeing the beginning and the end)** *as alluded to in the novel:* the belief that "God had planned for practically everybody before they were born a nasty surprise when they died." (Catholicism allows for a belief in **free will**.)

What are the five points of Calvinism (as gleaned from the Christian Bible)?

1. **Total depravity:** as a result of Adam's (mankind's) **"fall"** from grace, the entire human race is affected; all humanity is "dead" in its trespasses and sins - and man is not able to save himself.
2. **Unconditional election:** Because man is dead in sin, he is unable to initiate a response to God; it is God who has elected certain human beings to **salvation**; these people are God's **"elect"** add their being **predestined** is unconditional (no particular response from man is needed because man is unable to respond and, in fact, does not want to).
3. **Limited atonement**: Because **God has determined** that certain human beings should be saved unconditionally, he (God) has

determined that Christ should die for **the elect** alone and they alone will be **saved.**

4. **Irresistible grace**: God, through irresistible grace, draws to Himself those He elected (makes them willing to come to Him); when God calls, man responds.

5. **Perseverance of the saints:** Only the precise ones that God has elected and drawn to Himself through the Holy Spirit will persevere in faith and not be lost; they are eternally secure.

SESSION #22 OF THE TEACHER AND STUDENT IN LITERATURE ON PERSPECTIVE AND POLITICS IN THE PRIME OF MISS JEAN BRODIE

THE PRIME OF MISS JEAN BRODIE

Read: Chapters 4, 5, and 6 (to the end of the novel)

Prompts (Choose to respond to three of the six prompts below and email your thoughts to both Mr. Eidelberg and your course partner**):**

#1: It has been said (notice the passive voice) that one can get more than a whiff of fascism in Miss Jean Brodie in her prime: what do you say – and why? Where, specifically, do you think some readers would contend that they detect the stink?

#2: What surprises you about how the characters and the plot eventually play out?

#3: What are the various ways (plural!) that the concept of "perspective" figures in this novel?

#4: How does the author Muriel Spark make meaningful use of the literary technique of "time shift" to structure her novel?

#5: Where and how was the idea of "assassination" by betrayal first alluded to in the novel and how does in figure throughout the novel as a whole?

THE TEACHER AND STUDENT IN LITERATURE

#6: How do the different beliefs of Calvinism (a Protestant sect) and Roman Catholicism drive character and plot development in the story Muriel Spark tells?

Here are Hunter College student Anika Bradley's thoughts on the opening pages of Muriel Spark's THE PRIME OF MISS JEAN BRODIE and on the author's structured use of "time shift" in the service of characterization:

Prompt #1

During the first six pages of Muriel Spark's novel THE PRIME OF MISS JEAN BRODIE, Spark introduces the six girls Miss Brodie focuses on teaching and mentoring, the "Broodie set," through a flash forward into their teenage years. Spark introduces them as each being "famous" in the school and their close relationship with Miss Brodie, though she is no longer their teacher. Although the reader is not given much time to view Miss Brodie in action on these pages, as she only comes in on page 4 to whisk the girls away, we are given a lot of insight as to how she acts as a teacher based on the characterization of her top students. Spark illustrates that they are exceptionally intelligent students in fields the school was not keen on teaching, such as art, as the school has deemed it to be useless knowledge. Spark informs the reader that these six girls, as well as Jean Brodie, are "held in great suspicion" by other students and faculty at the girls' school (Spark 2). This could be because of how extremely elitist and private Miss Brodie and the set are with their company. Spark demonstrates this through new student Joyce Emily, who is trying to get in with the Brodie set, but Spark makes it very clear that will not happen. Miss Brodie dismisses her almost immediately upon her arrival.

At the end of these pages, Miss Brodie pulls her girls aside to tell them that somebody at the school is trying to get her to resign, and that this is not the first, and probably not the last, time this has happened, but that she will do no such thing. Through the brief interaction the reader has with Miss Brodie, it is easy to draw the conclusion that she is very set in her ways, and will only do things the way she wants them done, and expects that of her girls as well. As a reader, in these first pages, I did not feel like I was given enough of an individual perspective of each of the girls to characterize them accordingly. Spark writes what each of the girls is "famous" for in the school, but they are seen very much in their "set" exclusively on these pages. While Miss Brodie is hardly present in this introduction, the picture that is painted of her girls is much more focused on expanding Miss Brodie's character then it is about expanding each of the girls' individual personalities.

Prompt #2

The characterization of Jean Brodie as a schoolmarm type of teacher, a strict woman who believes she knows best for the six girls, is very consistent throughout the first three chapters. In the second half of chapter one, Miss Brodie takes her set outside to listen to her read poetry because she cannot teach what she wants to in the school because it is not in the curriculum. She tells all the girls to remain silent when Miss Mackay, the headmistress, comes to ask them what they are doing out there. She prides the girls for not answering the question put before them, thus disrespecting their headmistress, but Miss Brodie fully expects the girls to treat her with utmost respect as their teacher. Miss Brodie is a woman determined to create a group of girls who are the "crème de la crème." To Miss Brodie, that appears to mean a woman who puts goodness, beauty, and truth above everything. This is not all that surprising because during the first three chapters of the novel, that is exactly how the reader has seen Miss Brodie act. She does not show emotion often, and believes teaching her girls of famous painters and writers is more important than any science out there, thus showing her distaste of science teacher Miss Lockhart.

Muriel Spark sets the time shifts in the timeline of the novel to her advantage to provide the reader with the past and future of Jean Brodie and the Brodie girls. In chapter two, the reader is told by Eunice that Miss Brodie passed away after she resigned, and that it's a very long story, thus foreshadowing this story the reader is getting into. Euince also tells her husband that one of the girls betrayed Miss Brodie, thus leading to her untimely retirement. By having Euince share this information with her husband so many years into the future, it indicates to the reader that Eunice was *not* the one to betray Miss Brodie. Euince would have no logical reason to lie to her husband about betraying her former teacher, who he has never even heard of until this day. This could be a small hint of Spark's end that though we may not actually find out what the betrayal was or who did it until the end, we may be able to use the process of elimination through these flash forwards and flashbacks to determine who it *wasn't*.

Here are Hunter College student Khadiza Sultana's thoughts on the opening pages of Muriel Spark's novel THE PRIME OF MISS JEAN BRODIE and on the author's structured use of "time shift" in the service of characterization. These thoughts are then capped by her extra credit critical review of Ronald Neame's direction of the film version of Muriel Spark's novel:

Prompt: Whom does Spark make us meet on the first six pages of the novel and how are these characters presented to us (in what sequences and in what manner)? Did you expect to meet the title character first and right away? What are your first impressions of the key characters presented – and what do you base them on?

Unlike the average opening of a book, Spark introduces us to the titular character's pupils instead of the short novel's namesake. With the introduction of every girl, we learn a little bit about each one's fame and the way their hats sit atop their heads. Starting off this Brodie cult is Monica, a mathematical genius whose anger could leave those near her bruised left and right. She wears her hat higher that normal, much like that intelligence and anger of hers. Then there's Rose Stanley, the one famous for sex, but who wears her hat in a manner that does not draw attention to herself. Eunice Gardner is a petite girl well known for gymnastics and swimming. She wears her hat with the brim turned up, showcasing her face like that of a performer looking out to the audience after a grand somersault. Sandy is famed for her small eyes and English vowel pronunciation. Her hat is put as far back as possible on her head, held together by an ever-changing piece of elastic due to her chewing habits. Then there's Jenny, the prettiest and most graceful of the set and Sandy's best friend. She wears her hat with the brim bent sharply downward, the opposite of Eunice's hat-wearing manner and very much secured, unlike Sandy's hat. Last and seemingly the least in the eyes of the other characters is Mary, the silent nobody. Even the way she wears her hat is not described, not worth mentioning, like her presence.

I expected Spark to introduce Miss Jean Brodie in the beginning pages, perhaps starting out in her teaching career like Rick Dadier or reminiscing about the good old days like Mr. Chips. Spark gave neither as she focused on introducing each Brodie set member. Yet, through the overall descriptions of the set, we get a sense of what Miss Brodie may be like: eccentric, unconventional, an outcast. Maybe it's because I used the other teachers we've read about for comparison but doing so only made Miss Brodie's first appearance even more odd. Her opening line, "I have to consult you about a new plot which is afoot to force me to resign," comically made her out to be the head of a few hand-picked spies and assassins. Beyond those bits of dialogue, the overall impression I got from Miss Brodie is that she is a youthful soul stuck in the body of someone much older that she thinks and wants herself to be. She's strangely disciplined in that every time she finds her students distracted, she makes sure to snap them out of their daydreaming. Unprofessional and childlike enough to state that the greatest artist is who she prefers and obsessed with her prime, Miss Brodie encourages the girls to keep their actual lessons a secret and to pretend as though they are following the curriculum. Mary seems like the punching bag for the group, the one Miss Brodie could use as an example of what not to be. Constantly picked out of the flock to be belittled, the poor kid finds this period of her life to be happiest. Sandy seems to be the troubled smart student; I say this because of moments when she is told she "will go too far" and for times when her actions are guided in an overwhelming way by Miss Brodie's influence. Jenny gives off the impression of the rule-abiding, mannered one with the potential to become the crème de la crème. Eunice seems like the most outgoing, both physically with her flips and emotionally with her chattering nature. Monica didn't give me too strong of an impression and Rose seems like she was designed to be the seducer of the group, when she's really not.

Prompt: Where do these initial impressions get confirmed or rethought in the remainder of Chapter one as well as Chapter 2 and 3? What surprises you about how the characters and plot begin to play out - and why? Where is the idea of assassination by betrayal first introduced in the novel (either directly mentioned or implied), and how has the novel's "time shift" structure played a part in this?

For the remainder of Chapter 1 as well as Chapter 2 and 3, Spark gives more insight into Miss Brodie and Sandy. For all her peculiar antics, Miss Brodie has a strong sense of loyalty, one that she both preaches to her set and that she also exhibits when she scolds Rose for commenting on Miss Mackay's appearance. Even though Miss Brodie says plenty about Miss Mackay to the girls, allowing them to badmouth her would be disloyal to their union as teachers. Besides this, I gained a bit of appreciation for Miss Brodie due to her desire to expand her mind and the minds of her students. She wishes for them to grow into dedicated women, much in the way she had dedicated herself to them, albeit through unorthodox means.

She is still unprofessional and bizarre in that she continues to tell personal life stories to pass off as lessons, encourages her students to freely choose when she plans her own thoughts and biases into the girls, picks on Mary because she is the weakest, and even attempts to use Rose as her stand-in lover with Mr. Lloyd. Why a teacher would want to live her desires vicariously through her minor student, I don't know. It's strange that she would give up her affair with Mr. Lloyd but try to encourage such behavior from her student. Speaking of Rose, it feels off that she is known for *** when she is the least curious about it. If anything, Sandy and Jenny seem most preoccupied by that subject, Sandy especially, but in an unsettlingly way. She dislikes the idea of sex, but she likes Miss Brodie - possibly even more than what is appropriate for a student-teacher relationship. Sandy teeter-totters between admiration and disgust towards Miss Brodie and eventually this leads to her betrayal of her.

In the beginning, I tried to give all the characters the benefit of the doubt. Any one of these members could have betrayed Miss Brodie. Maybe it was Mary, and I think that if it was her, it would have been well-deserved. However, it turned out to be Sandy; there wasn't any build-up to this revelation either, it was like a passing comment. The novel's "time shift" structure is special in this way. We get exposed to little details concerning the Brodie set's lives in the future and how lasting an impact their teacher had on them. Though Sandy becomes a nun in the future, disappointing Miss Brodie's aspirations, she had been led to this route by her. I'm still trying to grasp how Sandy's obsession led to her betrayal. The first mention of assassination by betrayal occurs in our initial meeting with Miss Brodie; she discusses a plot being brewed against her and Spark compares her character with Julius Caesar. This earlier comparison should have ignited the idea that Sandy, the one closest to Miss Brodie, the one whose mind is possessed by Miss Brodie, would end up being the betrayer. Rather than "Et tu, Brute?" "Et tu, Sandy?" seems more fitting.

Dear Ronald Neame,

While many film adaptations stray completely from the original work's content, I felt that your movie did a good job in incorporating the basic plot points, which also were unique in its own way. However, it is this uniqueness that makes me question my knowledge of the characters and the story. In Spark's novel, we see the chinks in Miss Brodie's armor - the ways she fails as a teacher and as a general role model to her set, largely through the eyes of Sandy. In the film, Maggie Smith's portrayal of Miss

Brodie is truly admirable; it makes the watchers draw to her cult in the same way her own set had probably gravitated towards her in the novel.

Miss Brodie is always admonishing Mary for her stupidity, whereas the film molds that feature of her into a worthy teacher - one who truly leads and wishes to be a good guide to her students. It is because of Miss Brodie's treatment of Mary in the novel that Sandy also follows suit, falling into a moral dilemma of whether to be nice to her peer. Had this been illustrated in the film, watchers would have been able to see the problematic aspect of the Brodie set. We also don't see the effects of Miss Brodie on her set in their future. We don't get to see that the one she wanted as her replacement turned out to be rid of her influence completely, while the one she was betrayed by had been gripped by her influence the most.

It felt as though this film were just like any other movie about a "special" teacher, a portrait of her as a good disruption, someone who shook up the restrictive way of her students' thinking. The way she defended herself over the letter, which was also highlighted in the film's trailer, makes it seem as though Miss Mackay wrongfully accused Miss Brodie's character and teachings. Later when she shows her class pictures from her vacation and tearfully explains the story of Dante and Beatrice, she seems like a pitiful lover. Putting the two scenes together, one would assume Miss Brodie to be a truly dedicated and remarkable teacher whose students are above everything else, including her love life. But let's not be fooled by that. She attempts to reconcile her dedication to her prime with her obsession with Teddy Lloyd by making Jenny her proxy. Is she still a good teacher then? She rejects her lover – he's married and a Roman Catholic - but wishes to place her own student in her place because she just can't seem to let go.

The obsession seems romanticized and the inner moral turmoils of Sandy are downplayed in efforts to focus on the former. Speaking of Sandy, do you realize how simplified you made her obsession out to be? In one scene she tells Miss Brodie she is dependable and in the next scene they are together: the watcher can already assume the change in Sandy. In the film, it appears as though Sandy's beginning towards betrayal stems from being told that being emotional would be a handicap to her insight, and that morality cannot be applied to Jenny, who is destined to be a good lover. On one hand it can be presumed that this is the moment Sandy realizes that Miss Brodie isn't as morally good as she had seen her to be. On the other hand, it can also be assumed that jealousy and competition over a man are the large contributing factors in Sandy's dislike.

We never get to see or understand the little moments that lead up to the betrayal. For instance, film Miss Brodie changes her account of Hugh to match the artistry of Mr. Lloyd, but there's no reaction form Sandy. In the novel, Sandy is torn between her "admiration for the techniques and the pressing need to prove Miss Brodie guilty of misconduct." This is the same economy present in Mr. Lloyd's painting methods and later the very same principle she acts on for her betrayals. I feel that the watchers miss out on a great portion of Sandy's imagination, thoughts, and the information of her morals. It might also have been interesting to see the parallelism between Miss Brodie and Sandy in their own respective obsessions. Just as Miss Brodie couldn't stop hearing the same stories involving Mr. Lloyd, Sandy couldn't keep herself from asking Jenny time and time again about the female police officer. Just as Miss Brodie looked at Mr. Lowther possessively, so too did Sandy look in the same manner at Miss Brodie - the teacher she couldn't image falling from grace, who would engage in behaviors beneath her.

One thing I noticed in the beginning of the film was that when Miss Brodie was telling the girls that they did well in saying nothing, Sandy states that Miss Brodie had gone against her own words by making up a lie. It's interesting to see this coming from Sandy, when in the novel she doesn't speak against Miss Brodie's methods. Perhaps this was your attempt to plant a seedling in the minds of the watchers that from the very beginning, the one who would rise up against Miss Brodie and make her face the things she does would be Sandy. However, novel Sandy never spoke her mind against Miss Brodie, whereas film Sandy did. Film Sandy confronted Miss Brodie about all the wrong she had done, whilst novel Sandy never revealed herself as the assassin. Why that might be is up to interpretation. Overall, I thought that the movie was done well but that it possessed major differences in how the characters were portrayed and thus the kind of storyline it was forming.

Sincerely,

Khadiza Sultana

SESSION #23 OF THE TEACHER AND STUDENT IN LITERATURE ON MORALITY AND ETHICS IN THE PRIME OF MISS JEAN BRODIE

THE PRIME OF MISS JEAN BRODIE by Muriel Spark

It is essential that you complete your reading of Spark's short novel before you think about and write academically about the two prompts below. Also, you need to read the reader's question (but NOT YET the answer that follows it) in "The Ethicist" column that I recently sent you; stop reading where it says STOP, and then read what I'm about to tell you right now as background and context for much of the writing you will be doing for this session.

"The Ethicist" is a popular column that regularly appears in the Sunday magazine of the New York Times; for the past several years it has been written by a philosopher, Kwame Anthony Appiah, who is also a respected author of several books, a professor at NYU, and a practicing Muslim. The particular column I sent you is representative of the kinds of questions, concerns, problems, and quandaries about ethics and morality that appear in "The Ethicist" along with Professor Appiah's usually quite extended analyses and answers.

If you are wondering about the difference between ethics and morality, you are not alone, and a few years ago, Mr. Appiah offered his explanation (does it match your previous understanding of this distinction with a difference?):

> *"Morality" is sometimes used to refer to considerations having to do with how people should treat one another. "Ethics" (is sometimes used) to cover not just such moral considerations but also others that have do with human flourishing, with living a good life.*

Prompts (due to both Mr. Eidelberg and your course partner)

1. Based on your reading of THE PRIME OF MISS JEAN BRODIE, which questions, character actions, issues or situations in the novel are more in the realm of "ethics" (by the above definition and distinction)? Explain why you think so.
2. Based on your reading of THE PRIME OF MISS JEAN BRODIE, which questions, character actions, issues or situations in the novel are more in the realm of "morality" (by the above definition and distinction)? Explain why you think so.

CW/HW (due to both Mr. Eidelberg and your partner)

Pretend you are the Times's in-house ethicist and respond to the letter-writer as how specifically (and why) he should act. Then read Mr. Appiah's advice and reasons and add a P.S. to your letter dealing with how his advice and your advice differ (or not) and whether any particular difference has given you any second thoughts.

Here is Hunter College student Shelly Uzagir giving ethical advice as a New York Times columnist:

Dear Name Withheld,

That does sound like an "ethical quandary." I understand your hesitation towards telling your friend the real reason for the position rejection. Mainly because the reason was discussed in a private conversation between your wife and the department head. I will say, your friend is likely unaware of his "too full of himself" quality. I strongly believe in the importance of feedback and constructive criticism because shortcomings go unnoticed until they are called out. Your friend followed up with you numerous times because he genuinely wants to know what he did wrong. I think being transparent about his fault will allow him the chance to correct himself. If you stay silent about the matter, he will continue to make the same mistake and that'll prevent him from getting hired elsewhere. Make him aware so he knows to "turn the volume down," as you said. I understand that the department head may not want that information getting out, although, I am unsure why. I'd personally want to be honest with the denied candidate regardless of the reason (whether they're unqualified, unexperienced or trying to hard). I will never understand why professional people are so afraid of giving and receiving feedback. Nonetheless, I'd hope your friends would take the information (silently) to better himself rather than becoming defensive and argumentative. The department head should not hear back about the matter and if they do, I'd reconsider that friendship. Overall, if your wife is comfortable with you sharing the details of the conversation with your friend, in an effort to help him, I would proceed with passing along the information.

P.S. I agree with Mr. Appiah's advice and it seems like he would agree with me as well. To be transparent, I did not think that the "targeted hire" assumption was related to affirmative action. That statement adds to my point that if you don't inform your friend, he will continue to make the same mistake. Especially since he believes the rejection had nothing to do with his personality or qualifications. I also agree that there is an unwritten agreement of confidentiality in interviews – and private conversations. However, as Mr. Appiah mentioned, the chance to help your friend grow outweighs the breach of confidentiality.

I wish you the best.

Sincerely,

Shelly Uzagir

Here is Hunter College student Victoria Cecere giving ethical advice as a New York Times columnist:

To whom it may concern,

I'd like to start by thanking you for your submission to "The Ethicist." Though, this question is very difficult to answer because of the close-run between the loyalties to your wife's familiars compared to the loyalty you have toward your friend. On one hand, you want to be loyal to the person who might have said too much in confidence that you would not repeat it. Said confidentiality it is important because it distinguishes you as a person, as your ability to "keep your mouth shut" to put it bluntly is needed in this sort of situation. However, your friend would definitely benefit from your loyalty to them in telling them how they can better manage their interviewing skills for the next time they start to apply for other positions once again. My advice begins with asking you if there is a way to present the issue to your friend without putting the information or persons involved in the interview at risk. Instead, you would benefit from possibly using an alias of one of the other interviewees that was in the room at that time, as it is not likely that they will meet again at the same kind of setting. That, or you could benefit from asking them what they did in the interview, and try to polish any ill-fitting behavior that way. It would be pointless just to share the explicit information from the original interview, as that could eventually come back to haunt you and demean your character in the eyes of others. By using an alias or a mock-interview, you don't have to worry about your authenticity being challenged. You get to help your friend without harming your image or their trust in you. Instead, you are simply trying to help them out so they can try again. If they decide that they do not need your help, the fact that you tried is ethical enough. You kept your moral of loyalty alive by offering help, and kept your moral of confidentiality alive by not naming names or giving event-specific information. I hope this advice helps you regarding your decision, but this portion of the newspaper will always be open to other questions or concerns from readers such as yourself.

Thank you for your question and your support, it is appreciated!

Best,
Victoria C. (The Ethicist)

P.S.: I recently saw that the "The Ethicist" Kwame Anthony Appiah has given you an answer before I could send my message to you. While he does present the similar issue, and the need to uphold moral confidentiality, I feel as though he did not give you explicit instructions as to how to go about doing so. My suggestions of mock-interviewing or using the alias of someone who could have witnessed the bad behavior firsthand still stand. I think they are beneficial in appeasing both sides without causing you added stress. However, Mr. Appiah did well in unpacking both dilemmas equally, and helped you realize that you don't think they got a wrong impression of your friend. Interviews are definitely tough for people like your friend, because those few minutes of conversation will not give others the most accurate depiction of a person's character. Both anxiety and "interesting" personality types (both those that are too serious and those that are too comfortable) aid in the making or breaking of an impression. I would try to help your friend in those areas aswell, though it may be hard to come up with an introduction to such a lesson without offending them.

THE PRIME OF MISS JEAN BRODIE

(Please indicate at the bottom of this handout your priority order interest in participating in a small-group discussion and then front-of-the-room presentation on these five topics)

1. Ponder and try to make sense of this: when Mr. Eidelberg first taught this novel in the mid-1970's as a relatively new high school English teacher, he started off being greatly attracted to and wanting to be like Jean Brodie as a teacher, but by the end of several class discussions with his 11th-grade students he found that there was much about Miss Brodie that was both alienating and disturbing to him.

2. How do a society's norms (conventional values and standards) about love, sex, marriage, and parenting figure in this novel and how does the novel's depiction of these various human activities compare and contrast with the same behaviors in the other works of literature (including some popular films) that we have studied so far this term?

3. How dangerous today is the reality of a "cult of personality" in the societal areas of education, politics, government, religion, and family – and what do you think the Scottish author of this novel would say in answer to this question if she were alive today (she died ten years ago at the age of 88 in 2006)? As an intrinsic part of this same question, where do you see the idea of "playing God" in all this – and which characters in the novel might be seen as having auditioned for that role?

4. Jean Brodie says that she subscribes to the idea that a true "education" is what the word literally means in Latin: "a leading out (from)" and she insists that the Marcia Blaine School for Girls' Headmistress – Miss Mackay – is guilty of believing and implementing an opposite vision – namely that of "intrusion," an unsolicited and unwelcome insertion (into someone's mind) by others. Is Miss Mackay guilty as charged? Is Jean Brodie correct in her philosophical understanding of the essential nature of "education"? And is she faithful to that understanding – does Miss Brodie in her prime practice what she preaches?

5. It has been said of Miss Jean Brodie that, in her prime as a teacher, she was little more than the sum total of all her very quotable sayings (her maxims). To what degree is this true or not for the title character of Muriel Spark's most famous novel? In other words, what do all of Miss Brodie's

sayings about teaching, about learning, and about life mean to her and to the other human beings she comes in contact with -- and how do these maxims come together and add up to the person with the moral character and nature that we as readers of this novel either strongly love, or hate, or love to hate, or hate to love?

BONUS SESSION OF THE TEACHER AND STUDENT IN LITERATURE ON THE CULT OF PERSONALITY IN SCHOOL FICTION: JEAN BRODIE'S "SET" OF IMPRESSIONABLE GIRLS AND THE BOYS OF THE "DEAD POETS SOCIETY"

THE CULT OF PERSONALITY IN THE PRIME OF MISS JEAN BRODIE AND IN DEAD POETS SOCIETY

Read about what Mr. Eidelberg and others have to say about the unorthodox Miss Jean Brodie in her prime and "the cult of personality" in education on page 26 – 29 of SO YOU THINK YOU MIGHT LIKE TO TEACH. This section of the chapter ends with three paragraphs that all together contain a total of eight (8) questions raised by Mr. Eidelberg for the readers of his book (and those readers are now you).

Prompt: Explore as many of these eight questions as you like because they intrigue you, as well as any other questions that occur to you as you read over for the second time these cult of personality and "assassination" pages in SO YOU THINK YOU MIGHT LIKE TO TEACH. Also read for at least a second time the final five pages of the novel itself in order to mine them for questions they might raise for you that you would like to intellectually explore - page 133 beginning with "When Sandy returned" and ending with the quite famous last line of the novel (omitted from the movie version!): Sandy said: "There was a Miss Jean Brodie in her prime."

Alternate prompt: After re-reading the ending of the novel on page 133-137, watch on YouTube the 3 and ½ minute original trailer to the 1969 film version of THE PRIME OF MISS JEAN BRODIE plus the 10 and ½ minute concluding scene to the film version directed by Ronald Neame and told chronologically, without any time shifting and, also, with little religious content. Write a personal letter to director Ronald Neame discussing the changes to the novel's story and characterization that you can see, hear, and infer from these clips. (If you have the time and desire to view the wholes film, go for it!)

Two Separate Optional Extra Credit assignments due ONLY to Mr. Eidelberg:

1. On YouTube, experience another famous cult of personality story – the 1989 film DEAD POETS SOCIETY written by Tom Schulman (who later, in an unusual reverse sequence, adapted his film own script into an off-Broadway stage play) and starring Robin Williams as the teacher-personality. Either watch the short (2-minute) trailer and the whole film OR watch the extended four-minute trailer (Trailer #1 Classic Trailer) and two clips: the famous "seize-the-day" clip and the ending of the film clip. Send to Mr. Eidelberg ONLY – in any form of writing you choose – a piece of writing that expresses your thoughts and feelings about the nature of classroom cults of personality – their remarkable teachers and their susceptible students.

2. On YouTube, watch the trailer to the 1969 film version of THE PRIME OF MISS JEAN BRODIE, directed by Ronald Neame and starring the incomparable Maggie Smith. Write a letter to Mr. Eidelberg about two things: first, tell him whether you agree or disagree (and why) with his warning that students reading and studying Muriel Spark's novel should avoid watching the film version before they complete the book. Secondly, tell Mr. Eidelberg whether you think lovers of the novel should see the movie at all (either as an exploration from a different perspective of Jean Brodie's character and its influence on her chosen set of students or as a significant distortion of an important novel that is widely studied in high school and college English classes).

BONUS SESSION PROJECT: AN ORAL PRESENTATION ON REMARKABLE TEACHERS AND STUDENTS IN CHILDREN'S AND YOUNG ADULT LITERATURE

All of the literature selected by the instructor for this course on The Teacher and Student in Literature has as its audience the mature reader (people just like yourselves!). However, younger adults (like the adolescents you once were) have often met fictional teachers and students in literary works especially geared to them; in fact, young children (even juveniles) frequently met their first fictional classroom characters in books they were either able to read on their own or had read to them by their parents or their actual schoolteachers.

As college students in this course we should take a look – or a look back – at these works of literature (some of which may even be picture books). So, please choose from the curated list that follows (compiled with the help of a professional children's librarian who happens to be my sister) the title of a school-set work of literature created for readers and/or listeners ages infant to fifteen. Since no two students can report on the same work of literature, please get your first, second, and third preferences in to Mr. Eidelberg (in writing or by email) as soon as you can.

Then, after he has approved your choice of title, read your authorized work straight through in preparation for an oral presentation at the front of the room using only hand-held notes; you cannot read your presentation as a written report since you must make eye contact with your collegial audience except when you glance down to refer to or accurately quote from your notes; you will need to speak slowly, powerfully, and convincingly on the reasons you believe "the character" you read about for this project (a teacher, a student, a class, or a school even) can be considered "remarkable."

Your no-more-than-three-minute "brief" on this character's "remarkableness" (with an additional two minutes of questions and comments from the class and the instructor) will probably include mention of the character's persona, beliefs, thoughts, and actions and will benefit from actual sayings or words from the character's mouth (quotes) that embody the character's "remarkable" personality and pedagogical persona.

Prompts for both an oral presentation and a written extra credit assignment on:

TEACHERS (AND, OF COURSE, THEIR STUDENTS) IN CHILDREN'S AND YOUNG ADULT LITERATURE

(Where young readers meet their first fictional teachers)

Note: You will not find teachers from television and the movies in the list that follows; those teachers tend to be "bad": ignorant if not stupid when it comes to learning, lazy and looking to scam their classes or leave teaching, often clueless about, if not fearful of, kids, and so careless (care-less) that they couldn't care less about the consequences of their selfishness.

- What exactly (which particular action, reaction, thoughts, and remarks) make this fictional teacher *"remarkable"* as a teacher? What specifically about this teacher would cause him or her to be listed online as "memorable" or as a "favorite teacher" by mature adults looking back on the reading they did as either children or your adults (or on the listening they did if the book was read or shown to them as a picture book)? In still other words, *why might actual grown-ups wish they had had this fictional teacher for real* when they were in elementary school or junior or senior high school?
- Which positive and negative *attributes* and *qualities* and which *values, beliefs, ideals, and philosophies* as both a human being and a teacher does this fictional teacher *have in common* with

any of the several fictional teachers we have met and analyzed so far into his course on The Teacher and Student in Literature?

- Can you quote examples of **dialogue (conversation, announcements, proclamations, maxims, mottoes)** from your fictional teacher that capture the essence of that teacher as both a human being and as a working teacher?

The paraplegic teacher Mrs. Olinski and her sixth-grade class in THE VIEW FROM SATURDAY / E.L. Konigsburg

Ms. Bixby in MS. BIXBY'S LAST DAY / John David Anderson

Mr. Slinger in any of the books by Kevin Henkes that feature him

Mr. Falker in THANK YOU, MR. FALKER / Patricia Polacco

Mr. Ed McLeod, the gay student-teacher aspiring to be a regular teacher and his lover Paul, the uncle of McLeod's sixth-grade student, Archer, in THE BEST MAN / Richard Peck

Miss Nelson in **the three stories** that make up the MISS NELSON COLLECTION / Henry Allard

Miss Honey or Headmistress Trunchbull in MATILDA / Roald Dahl

Miss Frizzle in any one of the MAGIC SCHOOL BUS science education picture books (but not from the PBS television series) / Joanna Cole

Miss Tansy Culver (with a side glance at her predecessor, Miss Myrt Arbuckle) in THE TEACHER'S FUNERAL: A COMEDY IN THREE PARTS / Richard Peck

Miss Binney in RAMONA THE PEST / Beverly Cleary

The fifth-grader Nicholas and his relationship with his elementary school teacher in FRINDLE / Andrew Clements

The character of "School" in SCHOOL'S FIRST DAY OF SCHOOL / Adam Rex

Oliver's teacher in MY TEACHER FOR PRESIDENT / Kay Winters

Miss Agnes in Alaska in THE YEAR OF MISS AGNESS / Kirkpatrick Hill

Mr. Terupt in BECAUSE OF MR. TERUPT / Rob Buyea

Arthur's school assignment experiences in ARTHUR'S TEACHER TROUBLE or in ARTHUR WRITES A STORY / Marc Brown

Arthur's younger sister's experiences in D.W.'S GUIDE TO PRESCHOOL / Marc Brown

Mr. Isobe in CROW BOY / Taro Yashima

Miss Bonker (and the other rule-breaking teachers) in HOORAY FOR DIFFENDOOFER DAY / Dr. Seuss (with Jack Prelutsky and Lane Smith)

The *"Me Project"* teacher who leaves teaching in JUDY MOODY WAS IN A MOOD / Megan McDonald

SESSION #24 OF THE TEACHER AND STUDENT IN LITERATURE ON BEL KAUFMAN'S 1964 NOVEL UP THE DOWN STAIRCASE

UP THE DOWN STAIRCASE

This uniquely structured American work of literature was published in hardcover in 1964 as a 12-part, 58-chapter novel (yes, 58 short chapters!); however, it was originally composed three years earlier in 1961 as a 3 and ½-page self-contained story that some popular magazine might potentially buy and print. According to an introduction its author Bel Kaufman especially wrote for the 1991 softcover edition of UP THE DOWN STAIRCASE, Kaufman's original magazine story was initially rejected by several magazine editors before finally being published by "The Saturday Review" magazine in late 1962 under the title "From a Teacher's Wastepaper Basket.")

So what was it that came across to editors as "weird-looking" visually and "too-different" in the curves of its narrative arc (though the novel was later positively advertised on its inside front cover with the sentence "Nothing quite like it has ever been written")?

Here's what: Kaufman **composed** both her original story and her later 340-page hardcover novel **from various kinds of written communications** ("papers") that she **ironically juxtaposed** (placed one right *after the other to make or call attention to a larger point*). These "papers," the author wrote in her introduction to the softcover edition, were her way of telling "a story of chaos, confusion, cries for help, bureaucratic gobbledygook" in an inner-city school and of one "newbie" New York City high school English teacher's attempt "to make a difference" in the lives of her students. (The novel is highly autobiographical, with Sylvia Barrett as a fictional stand-in for Bel Kaufman.)

Although unique in its structure (the makers of the 1967 Hollywood movie based on the 1964 novel, and starring a quirky Sandy Dennis, couldn't really figure out how to recreate that specific structure), Kaufman's novel UP THE DOWN STAIRCASE is interestingly related to the first novel studied in this course, THE BLACKBOARD JUNGLE by Evan Hunter, in its content, its setting, its themes, and its teacher and student relationships.

As you read this somewhat-long but fast-reading novel over the next week and a half, do BOTH of the following activities (there is no writing to do tonight):

First, choose one of the student characters in the novel and become him or her to the extent that you *start and keep* a "Here I am! Care about me!" personal journal or diary in that student's name about his or her life as a resident of New York City and a student in a large New York City high school.

Kaufman characterizes (paints portraits of) such key student types as: "the class comedian," "the sycophantic politician," "the over-ripe girl bursting with sexuality," "the black boy with a chip on his shoulder," "the Puerto Rican boy who finds himself," "the silent girl who doesn't find herself." Feel free to become anyone (but only one) of these students (or any other student in the novel, regardless of gender compatibility) and, in your writing, turn that type into an individual human being.

Secondly (but simultaneously with your journal/diary keeping), notice Kaufman's use of categories of "paper" as the "building blocks" of her novel's narrative arc and immediately begin to keep a list of the **page numbers in paragraph locations** that your favorite building blocks appear on.

By the way, according to Kaufman, almost all of these building blocks were *made up by her*: they are not really from actual school "papers"; nevertheless, they are truly believable as "for real," as many of you who are currently teachers can probably attest to. Some of the categories of "paper" building blocks that you will easily notice are:

- Memos (memorandums) filed away in desk drawers or wastebaskets;
- Items in the Calvin Coolidge High School newspaper;
- bulletin board items on the walls of the school's corridors;
- faculty conference minutes;
- a teacher's lesson plan;
- a student's minutes on a teacher's lesson;
- a chairperson's evaluative comments on a teacher's lesson;
- directives (to teachers) from school administrators;
- reports (to teachers) from school administrators;
- suggestions from students found in Miss Barrett's suggestion box;
- sentences or paragraphs from letters or notes (between friends, between colleagues, between teachers and students).

INTRODUCTION TO THE 1964 NOVEL UP THE DOWN STAIRCASE BY BELL KAUFMAN

Bel Kaufman's quite unusually structured and fairly long novel is the book end of our course that began with Evan Hunter's conventionally structured and also fairly long novel THE BLACKBOARD JUNGLE. Both are set in the urban classrooms of New York City in the 1950's; both were written by native New Yorkers (one Jewish, one Italian) who possessed New York City teaching licenses and had taught in that city's classrooms as English teachers; both had Hollywood movies quickly made after their novels proved enormously popular with American readers. (Mr. Eidelberg is not a fan of the movie of UP THE DOWN STAIRCASE because he finds the performance of its leading actress, Sandy Dennis, unfaithful to the unique qualities of teacher Sylvia Barrett in the novel. Also, what is quite special about the structuring of Kaufman's novel has no cinematic equivalent in the movie's conventionally told story.) While the next four or so concluding sessions of our course will be devoted to UP THE DOWN STAIRCASE, some former students in The Teacher and Student in Literature have wondered whether it might have been better to start the course with UP THE DOWN STAIRCASE and end it with THE BLACKBOARD JUNGLE, and you might like to keep this question in mind and weigh in on it as you read Bel Kaufman's book.

So, and also as an integral part of this session, first read in SO YOU THINK YOU MIGHT LIKE TO TEACH as a remote introduction to the entire novel (which normally I would have conducted on campus as part of a full-class discussion, but so be it) all of Chapter 8 (a case study devoted solely to this novel and its students, teachers, subject supervisor, and school administrators) on pages 115-131).

Then read as many of the opening "parts" of the novel as you reasonably can without stressing yourself out, but do try your best to make it through at least Part III; handle the following prompts on the basis of only those parts that you have actually read:

Prompt: Read Chapter 1 OUT LOUD to someone you are sheltered at home with (or OUT LOUD to yourself). Author Bel Kaufman explicitly intended for you to do this. What thoughts and feelings do you get and have as a result of this oral and auditory experience? Why do you think Kaufman wanted to create these feelings and thoughts in you at the very start of her novel?

Prompt: Verbally, UP THE DOWN STAIRCASE opens with the words "Hi, Teach." Author Bel Kaufman has written that as soon as she began to create UP THE DOWN STAIRCASE as a novel (from a rejected 3 and 1/2 – page short story magazine submission), she knew how she would end the novel (her first and, it turned out, only one). Predict (don't peek!) how a novel that opens with "Hi, teach" might intend to end.

Prompt: Kaufman has written about her novel: "Ironically juxtaposed, these pages told a story of chaos, confusion, cries for help, bureaucratic gobbledygook, and one teacher's attempt to make a difference in the life of a youngster." Give one example from the novel of where this statement is vividly true (for you) and how the structure of the novel helped to produce its effects on you.

SESSION #25 OF THE TEACHER AND STUDENT IN LITERATURE ON THE "HEY, TEACH" OF UP THE DOWN STAIRCASE

UP THE DOWN STAIRCASE

Continue your reading of Bel Kaufman's novel.

On YouTube, view the 4 and ½ minute Official Trailer to the Hollywood film version of the novel UP THE DOWN STAIRCASE.

Required Prompt #1: Based on your viewing of the movie trailer (watch it at least twice), how has the film version of Bel Kaufman's unconventional novel UP THE DOWN STAIRCASE been made into a disappointingly conventional Hollywood movie? Be specific about actual "conventions" (perhaps you should check out that word's meanings and uses). Of course, feel free to watch the entire film if you have the time and inclination.

On YouTube, view (at least twice) the 3 and ½-minute clip that can be found only by typing in "Up the Down Staircase + A Tale of Two Cities" on the YouTube search line; in this clip, actress Sandy Dennis, as English teacher Sylvia Barrett, teaches a literature study lesson on the Charles Dickens novel A TALE OF TWO CITIES (whereas the Sylvia Barrett of the novel, who is actually a somewhat fictionalized version of author Bel Kaufman, taught a lesson on a Robert Frost poem).

Required Prompt #2: Pretend you are the English chairperson in the back of the classroom, there to officially observe and evaluate Sylvia Barrett teach and them to write up a formal observation repost. Pay particular attention to the substantive content of the lesson, the quantity and quality of the teacher's questions, the engagement of the students in the lesson (and with the teacher and with one another), and the lesson's timing and pacing. Then write the lesson up; include specific commendations about what you saw and heard, specific recommendations (suggestions for improvement), and a overall rating of either superior, very favorable, favorable, satisfactory, or unsatisfactory.

Required CW/HW (both "a" and "b"): Since the existence of a Suggestion Box is one of the notable strengths of Sylvia Barrett's overall strength as a high school teacher of English, do both of the following creative writing activities:

    a. Pretend to be one of the students in Miss Barrett's English class or homeroom class (official class) and write out a specific suggestion for insertion in Miss Barrett's suggestion box. (Do not sign the suggestion, but do let Mr. Eidelberg and your course partner know which student you are currently pretending to be for your diary/journal writing writing, which you should be well into at this point.

    b. Pretend you are the particular you that you were when you were high school student - and then write as that you a specific suggestion for one of your actual high school English teachers for insertion in that teacher's classroom suggestion box.

Here is how Hunter College student Anika Bradley responded as one of Miss Barrett's students on the installation of a classroom suggestion box:

I like this idea of suggestion box. Most teachers here don't really listen to us enough. Miss Egan in the nurse's office is a joke, only tea and a pitying glance from her. I've heard Mrs. Schachter is okay, but I've never met her. You're new here, so I hoped you might be different from all of the others, but you have a non-skippable meeting so I'm writing this instead. I don't know, maybe I was wrong. I'll figure it out, I guess.

Here is how Hunter College student Jessica Chu (aka "Glasses" in her earlier high school days) time-travel responded to prompt "b":

Can we please slow down on some of these lessons? I know you said that class averages were down for the recent test but I think most of us are still very lost and confused about the lessons. I suggest that it is possible we split into group work of 3-5 so we may discuss amongst ourselves before checking with you that our work is indeed correct. Towards the end of class we could reconvene and go over everything together. I find this to be more helpful than solo work. We already have group discussions during our lunch period but it would be helpful if you were there too to help us and correct us. Thank you!

–Glasses

Here is how Hunter College student Rifath Islam (first as student "Mr. X" and then as her earlier high school self) handled the fictionally for real and retrospectively actual suggestion boxes of CW/HW parts "a" and "b":

I like your class you are a very good teacher and you make me want to learn even if I don't really want to. You are a good role model but I do not like the way that you keep giving exams just because everyone else says so. I didn't study for the last one and got a 89, but I studied for this one and almost failed. It speaks for itself.

(Mr. X)

To Mr. Brooks,

I appreciate that you try to keep grading fair and realistic, but I think it's a little unfair that you limit the pages of our essays. I also think it was a little bit unfair that you did not accept any new themes of a novel besides what you discuss in class, it takes away the idea of creativity.

Respectfully,
Rifath I.

SESSION #26 OF THE TEACHER AND STUDENT IN LITERATURE ON THE STYLE AND THE STUDENTS OF UP THE DOWN STAIRCASE

UP THE DOWN STAIRCASE

Work long and hard to complete your reading of the novel for this session.

STAYING AFTER SCHOOL

Read all of Chapter 5 in Mr. Eidelberg's text STAYING AFTER SCHOOL for insights into Bel Kaufman's writing of her only novel. This chapter largely deals with Kaufman's structuring of "pieces of paper" into the building blocks of UP THE DOWN STAIRCASE, and you will also get insight into Kaufman's writing and characterizing style, as well as her overall attitude, tone, and wit (which, regrettably, the Hollywood movie version of the novel rarely captures).

Read (optional) all of Chapter 6 of STAYING AFTER SCHOOL to see how previous on-campus students in this course brought Sylvia Barrett and another teacher from a different work of course literature together for an extended in-person conversation, an exchange of letters or emails, a telephone call, or some other form of correspondence or one-on-one communication.

For extra credit, do something similar (a playlet or a scene or two) either on your own or working together with your course partner; email the resultant piece of creative dialogue writing to Mr. Eidelberg within the next two weeks.

Prompts (all due now to Mr. Eidelberg and your course partner):

(a) your series of diary entries or personal journal entries as one of the adolescent students in UP THE DOWN STAIRCASE

(b) from your ongoing list of pages from the past several sessions containing "pieces of paper" that Bel Kaufman used to serve as the glue of her novel, a brief written explanation of why one of them is your favorite from the entire novel

(c) make up one of your own such "piece of paper" ("trivia in duplicate") based on both your reading of all the ones that, in fact, Kaufman fabricated (with just a few exceptions!) and your experiential knowledge of the administration of American public high schools

Required CW/HW ("in-voice" writing due now to Mr. Eidelberg and to your course partner):

Give a second reading to pages 50 top to 51 middle of Mr. Eidelberg's text STAYING AFTER SCHOOL. Then, pretend that you are a newbie teacher, like Sylvia Barrett, listening to Principal Clarke's welcome speech to his faculty on the teachers' first day back from summer vacation. Write an anonymous letter to Principal Clarke (you can call yourself "Ann Nonymous") telling him what you think of and feel about his words of welcome to the profession of teaching and its execution at Calvin Coolidge High School.

Optional CW/HW:

Be the Hunter College student you actually are now and write to your earlier "up-the-down-staircase" high school self a letter offering helpful looking-back advice, or words of wisdom, or consoling empathy or sympathy. Of course, be sure to "let it be a challenge" to you.

Here is how Hunter College student Anika Bradley explained her choice of certain letters from parents as her favorite "pieces of paper" comprising UP THE DOWN STAIRCASE:

My favorite "piece of paper" from the novel are the letters from the parents in regards to Open School Day (pages 203-204). The lack of interest the parents showed in their children's education and academic development surprised me. It's not all that surprising when students aren't concerned with reading, writing, or spelling. However, I certainly can't blame the students for wanting to drop out with such unapologetically, unbothered parents.

For example, Elsie Paine was more concerned with her daughter's appearance than her academic performance. In addition, Bess Martin suggested that Miss Barrett overlook her son's spelling deficiency. Furthermore, Lucile Rosen requested Miss Barrett's assistance with finding out who her daughter has been hanging out with after school. I believe this "piece of paper" reflects the ultimate outcome of the students' decisions in regards to their future.

Here is how Hunter College student Rifath Islam both responded to Principal Clarke's welcome letter and explained her choice of all of Chapter 41 of UP THE DOWN STAIRCASE as her favorite "piece of paper" from the novel:

Dear Principal Clarke,

Thank you for your welcome message – I look forward to teaching the wonderful students of Calvin Coolidge High School. I am unsure that my education has prepared me to shoulder the burdens and responsibilities of this miniature democracy. There are some things, like teaching, where experience has proven to be the strongest weapon. Nevertheless, I am a "mature and thinking citizen," therefore I am quite ready to execute my job and provide the students with a well-rounded education.

You stated that in this school we (teachers) are proving ourselves worthy and deserving of your trust and expectations. I understand that as principal you are relying on teachers to instruct and educate young adults. I also understand there is an expectation for teachers to demonstrate an impact on student's learning through test scores and/or observed practices. However, I believe we (teachers) must prove ourselves worthy to the students as they are the ones whose trust we must earn and expectations we must meet. I intend to speak with my students directly to learn what they want and need from me. I must say, your speech sounded like one from the current leader of the free world rather than the leader of Calvin Coolidge High School. Regardless, I understand the objective.

Best,

Ann Nonymous

Of all the pieces of paper that Kaufman compiles to make up her novel, my favorite has to be the entirely of "Chapter 41 – Do You Plan to Indulge in a Turkey?" My older sister is a new teacher, she tells me about the struggles that she experiences in the classroom every day. Reading this chapter is what really made this story feel most like it's a real teacher who's narrating the struggles of being a new teacher. The beginning of the Miss Barrett's written letter to Ellen showed a classroom that was slowly accepting Miss Barrett as a teacher – there was still chaos indicated in the lesson, but I was a particular fan of how Miss Barrett took to shaping her lesson around her students, urging them to get their thoughts out in a letter rather than making the class follow a robotic lesson. After that, the readers see almost a complete shift in the students, as they went absolutely "buck wild" in the cafeteria destroying things and we saw a natural authoritative response from Mr. McHabe in which he immediately tries to punish all the students responsible for the mess in the café, but decides against it as he realizes "punishing many for the misdeeds of a few was not only undemocratic, but would likely lead to another "unwarranted outburst." This particular part is what I was most taken with, as I found it interesting in the way authority figures operated, whether they would take action because they wanted change or just simply to punish. It seemed initially that Mr. McHabe wanted to punish but decided against it purely because of the later chaos that would ensue. He did not seem to care about *why* the students were acting out but was more concerned about the consequences that it caused. The following parts of the chapter were simply just heartwarming, to see the class collectively wish Miss Barrett a Happy Thanksgiving and seeing the shift in character when they're not in the classroom. It helped show readers that perhaps students have more to them than how they act in a classroom and the scene reminded me a lot of the closing scene in "To Sir, With Love," in which all the students collectively showed their thanks to Sir during the dance.

Here is how Hunter College student Rifath Islam handled the looking-back letter of advice extra credit assignment:

To my younger self,

High school is a rollercoaster – it's cliché, but it's true. And it doesn't last forever, which I think is one of the more important things to remember. Looking back on those four years, there are a lot of points of highs and lows (and middles). You know all those people who say that junior year almost always changes everything? Yeah, they're right – or at least in our case, they're right. The first two years will be fine, easy-flowing. You'll get comfortable with your friends and there will be many points in which you're sure of yourself, which is a great thing. There'll be moments when you're not too sure of yourself, which is also normal, but keep in mind that moments like those don't always last, that's why it's always so important to cherish them when you have them. Unfortunately, those friends you have won't last, but don't worry, it'll be a bittersweet realization and you'll be okay in the end! It's important for you to keep up with your schoolwork at all times, though! It's very important that you don't lose sight of that because I know you already know that nothing should really get in the way of your future.

Junior year will be a bit messy, but I promise it'll be fine, and you'll get through it (spoiler, you get straight A's!). The rocky year will give you leeway into a pretty great senior year! And this is when you find your new friends who will stick with you for years afterward. It'll be fun, the last year of high school will pass in a blur and it'll be a little sad, but on to college! You go to Hunter College – it wasn't your first choice, but you don't spend too much time beating yourself up because now you know how to pick yourself up after a few falls. Your first year will be a bit hectic, there's just going to be a lot going on, but you get through that too. Then 2020 will hit and it'll be a crazy rollercoaster, a very not easy transition into at-home learning, and some pretty bad moments here and there, but you always find something to cheer yourself up with because you made it into the nursing program! By August, you've adjusted to this whole online course thing, you're making sure you're safe, and you're making new friends despite the hurdles that were thrown in your way.

This all being said, it's important to remember through all of it that if there's anyone who knows how to stand back up after a fight well fought, it's you! It's easy to lose hope, to want to give up when the going gets a little tough the first time around, but it only gets easier with time. And it's important for you to know that you can fight for what you want, it's okay, don't be discouraged! Life won't always be easy, but you'll learn to play the cards that life deals you – even if they're not the greatest. You'll make it through every fight, and it'll be worth it in the end! Good luck, you got this!

Sincerely,

Your older self

Here is how Hunter College student Lisa Baez kept the diary of UP THE DOWN STAIRCASE student Elizabeth Ellis:

Dear Diary,

Yesterday was my first day of school. There is a new English teacher this term, and she seems nice so far. I think she will be a good fit for the school. I'm so excited to see how she will treat us and how things will turn out. I think that she will be my last hope for improving my writing. I'm really hoping for her to like me – if not, it will be a disappointment. Besides, if the school get worse and not better, I might quit school for good. I do want to learn, but I've had enough – I will no longer tolerate bad teachers whose intentions are not the best of our interest.

Sincerely,

Elizabeth Ellis

Dear Diary,

Today, I had the opportunity to meet with my English teacher, Miss Barrett, after school. She is really an incredible teacher; she is the first teacher ever that has shown me that she cares about us; she seems eager to teach us. I like that she encourages me to write more. I'm trying my hardest to improve my writing; however, I know that Miss Barrett can't give me her full attention since other students have the same problems as me. In all honesty, this makes me feel sad because I feel like I'm wasting my time.

Sincerely,

Elizabeth Ellis

Dear Diary,

Miss Barrett has come up with the idea that we should give her suggestions on everything that could help us achieve our goal – she put in a suggestion box, which is where we will place our suggestions. I think she cares about what we think and feel. She even allows us to write about personal things in the suggestion box. I believe that all my classmates are looking up to Miss Barrett even though they don't admit it. Everyone can agree with me that she has been amazing so far. I'm hoping she stays here for next term.

Sincerely,

Elizabeth Ellis

Dear Diary,

Today, I had an amazing day at school. I am enjoying Miss Barrett's writing assignments because they allow me to think critically. Besides, I got my writing assignment titled "A Comparative Study" back from Miss Barrett and, she commented, "Excellent, as always!" This fills me with joy because this means that I'm making progress in my writing. I must say, Miss Barrett has helped me a ton with my improvement. Therefore, I want to keep on doing a good job and keep proving to her that I'm a good writer.

Sincerely,

Elizabeth Ellis

Dear Diary,

I'm hoping for Miss Barrett to be teaching Creative Writing next term. I genuinely enjoy having her as a teacher, and I would not choose any other teacher over her. Miss Barrett provides me with good life lessons. Besides that, I know that she could help me become a future writer. I haven't shared this with anyone, but writing is truly my passion and I want to be good at it. I'm really hoping that she teaches Creative Writing next term – it could be extremely beneficial for me.

Sincerely,

Elizabeth Ellis

Here is Hunter College student Shelly Uzagir writing an UP THE DOWN STAIRCASE diary as the student Vivian Paine:

Dear Diary,

I have a new English teacher, her name is Miss Barrett. She is pretty, thin and a good dresser - overall very attractive. Her appearance reminds me of my sister. She also seems fair and understanding, similar to Mrs. Schachter. I told Miss Barrett about Mrs. Schachter when she asked us what we got out of English so far. I think she will treat us justly. It seems like she cares about our opinions and might like us. I hope she doesn't leave. My mom would like her, she's so skinny!

Dear Diary,

Miss Barrett put in a suggestion box – she really cares what we think! I think she is a teacher that's like a friend, but I'm not sure. I want to tell her about my personal issue, but I don't think she'd want to hear it. I once told Miss Friedenberg about my problem, I don't think she cared. None of the teachers like me. Except Miss Barrett, I think she might like me. I wish I was skinny like Miss Barrett and my sister. Maybe I should try to lose some weight. I would probably look just like her!

Here is Hunter College student Jessica Chu's version of Jose Rodriguez's personal journal over the course of several months:

Sept.

New teacher today. She's pretty too. I wonder if she's gonna be one of the good English teachers. Maybe she will quit soon too.

Oct.

Today Miss Barrett introduced a suggestion box. She asked about our English class experiences and I have nothing good to say. Only one teacher cared and didn't get me in trouble. That was nice. Miss Barrett didn't even make us sign our names but I ended it signed by "Me."

Oct.

It's my birthday today! Dad's working and I have to take care of the house so no one cares but me. I wished myself a Happy Birthday in the Suggestion Box. I wonder if she even knows my name.

Oct.

Wow. Miss Barrett HAS to be the best teacher ever! Today I got to play the judge in English class. The other day she asked me to play the judge so today I showed up in a black graduation gown and mortarboard borrowed from Denny downstairs. Since I was the judge of course I had to bring a hammer to "Order in the Court"! I played my role perfectly today. I feel like a changed person. I've never felt so confident and never received so much respect from my classmates. Whenever I talked, there was silence. Whenever there was a challenge, I was able to overrule every objection. Things are starting to look up for me. I have to start learning more from Miss Barrett. I have to thank her for this opportunity. I really like her. I feel like she actually cares and wants us to learn. Maybe I'll stay in school for longer, become a lawyer even!

Nov.

I really like Miss Barrett's class. We talked about race, we talked about the importance of grades. Her classes are never boring and she makes things easy to understand. I even got a Library Card and asked Miss Barrett for more reading suggestions. I hope to have her again. I really feel like I can learn in her class.

Dec.

Miss Barrett hurt her leg and is currently in the hospital. I hope she's doing ok. We all wrote to her today and I told her that I view her fondly and love her like my own mother. I hope she comes back soon. Classes without her just drag on and aren't the same. Did I ever enjoy class this much?

143

SESSION #27 OF THE TEACHER AND STUDENT IN LITERATURE ON HOW HOLLYWOOD MADE BEL KAUFMAN'S UNIQUE SCHOOL NOVEL INTO A CONVENTIONAL MOVIE

UP THE DOWN STAIRCASE

Prompt #1: Based on your viewing of the movie trailer, how has the film version of Bel Kaufman's unconventional novel UP THE DOWN STAIRCASE been made into a disappointingly conventional Hollywood movie?

Here is how Hunter College student Jessica Chu handled the conventional way in which the novel UP THE DOWN STAIRCASE was filmed:

Bel Kaufman's novel UP THE DOWN STAIRCASE is unconventional because it does not adhere to the standard format of literature. The novel does not have narration, rather it is formatted as bits of communication. The story is told through a collection of letters to Sylvia's friend Ellen, intra-school communications, pieces of students' assignments, their notes from the suggestion box, etc.

In addition, UP THE DOWN STAIRCASE does not contain certain elements of a conventional plot, such as rising action and falling action. Undoubtedly, it's not possible to transfer the unconventional format of the novel to the Hollywood movie. Therefore, the trailer depicted narration, verbal communication and real-time physical action. Furthermore, the movie seems to include the five standard plot elements: exposition, rising action, climax, falling action, and resolution. The Hollywood movie checks all the conventional boxes – agreeably disappointing, but ultimately unavoidable.

Here is how Hunter College student Anika Bradley handled the conventional way in which the novel UP THE DOWN STAIRCASE was filmed:

Bel Kaufman's novel UP THE DOWN STAIRCASE is an unconventional novel because of the stylistic choices in which it was written. Kaufman does not write scenes the way a traditional novelist would, with dialogue, a setting, a specific starting and ending time, etc. She chose to hardly write scenes at all, instead portraying the chaos of the school Miss Sylvia Barrett teaches in through memos between teachers and faculty, suggestion notes from students, staff meeting minutes, lesson plans, students' written work, letters from Sylvia to her friend Ellen, and more.

The unconventional nature of this novel and reliability on paper makes it nearly impossible to turn into a movie, at least one that properly reflects the novel in any way aside from the basic plotline. The movie version of UP THE DOWN STAIRCASE is conventional and traditional, as it has to be. A movie would be hard to film without dialogue or settings, only things strictly taking place on paper. A "conventional" Hollywood movie could be described as a classic narrative with a linear timeline where the viewer is a third party looking onto the scene, but not a part of it (hence the "fourth wall" of acting). A "conventional" novel could also have an incredibly similar definition, which does not fit as well with the novel of UP THE DOWN STAIRCASE. I would be interested to see if a filmmaker could capture the chaotic nature of the novel in a movie, but I believe it's unlikely and would be incredibly difficult.

Here is how Hunter College student Rifath Islam handled the conventional way in which the novel UP THE DOWN STAIRCASE was filmed:

The trailer of the movie seems very focused on the hectic classroom setting, alongside being very focused on the idea of a struggling new teacher in an new setting, which is what Kaufman's novel is mainly focused on. However, this trailer slightly diverged from the novel in that it took the conventional Hollywood route, rather than focus what Kaufman was truly trying to tell in the novel, which is the struggles of students in a classroom and how much of a real problem it is, even in real life. Instead, this trailer seems to romanticize many aspects of the novel, not truly giving focus to the main idea of the story, which is a pretty typical thing of Hollywood to do, in order to drive interest in the movie. Many "conventional" ideas in Hollywood include a chronological, predictable plot with the end of the film containing a "solution" to the conflict presented in the film. Additionally, there are many clichés that are also involved in Hollywood that, while many attempt to diverge from it now, was still very much present in older movies such as this once. That being said, I think the director of "Up the Down Staircase" turns this novel into a "disappointingly conventional Hollywood movie" by using these ploys in the film, such as the idea of the teacher fixing the problems of all the students and seemingly presenting a "happy ever after" at the end. However, the film barely seems to acknowledge the bigger picture that Kaufman was trying to emphasize by leaving out major conflicts that the students face by focusing primarily on the teacher, herself. The layout of the novel was presented through memos for a reason, to give the illusion of a real story, but the way that the film is portrayed in this trailer, it largely diverges from Kaufman's perspective of the novel.

Here is how Hunter College student Jessica Chu formally observed the lesson Sylvia Barrett taught in the film version of UP THE DOWN STAIRCASE:

Today I observed Sylvia Barrett conduct a lesson on the novel A TALE OF TWO CITIES by Charles Dickens. Miss Barrett instructed a student to read the first paragraph out loud while the other students followed along. When the student finished reading, she asked the class, "What strikes you immediately?" A few students answered quickly, "the differences, the contrasts, the opposites."

Miss Barrett advised the class that when two opposites are used together for contrasting effect, it is called antithesis. Miss Barrett then asked another student to read the next phrase. She then posed the question, "Can we still say that today, is it still the best of times, is it still the worst of times?" Numerous students responded that it is just the worst of times because of poverty, dangerous parks, and narcotics. Miss Barrett made a point to say there is also prosperity and new developments. She did this to remind the students that although there are bad things, there are also good things in the works. The majority of the class was eager to join the discussion.

Overall, I think Miss Barrett did a wonderful job asking questions that allowed the students to think critically. In addition, she engaged her students using literature and I was impressed by the class participation.

However, I do have a suggestion for keeping order in the classroom. Please consider making hand raising an enforceable rule. I noticed that when you allow students to shout out their answers, you are unable to address each response. In addition, the classroom became noisy in the midst of the discussion and I was unable to hear (or think about) each student's answer. It is important for the students to learn from you, but they must also learn from each other. With everyone speaking above one another, it is quite difficult to do that. To conclude, I think Miss Barrett did a wonderful job and her students genuinely learned from the lesson. My overall rating is favorable.

Prompt: Pretend you are the English chairman in the back of the classroom, there to observe and evaluate Sylvia Barrett teach and then to write up a formal observation report; write the lesson up with specific commendations and specific suggestions for improvement, and give the lesson an overall rating.

Here is how Hunter College student Anika Bradley formally observed as "overall favorable" a lesson that Sylvia Barrett taught in the film version of UP THE DOWN STAIRCASE:

1. Excellent job beginning the lesson by having a student read the novel being discussed, ensuring any student who did not come prepared for class is now caught up and engaging the students in the reading and listening to classmates rather than listening to you read to them. Reading only small sections at once, as you did, is also smart to be sure students do not begin to nod off.

2. Turning students' first impression thoughts into the formal concepts (example, antithesis) was smart, showing them they have the right ideas and advancing those ideas further. Showing them moments of praise is essential for boosting classroom confidence and showing them you are open to all their ideas, you did that very well.

3. Moving about the room, in between students and to different chalkboards, is key for facilitating student involvement and participation. I commend you for having that skill down strategically instead of looking as though you're running around the room.

4. Relating their current life experiences back to the novel written more than 100 years ago is essential, and you did that well, Miss Barrett.

5. Good job in showing the students that the present could still be considered "the best of times" and "the worst of times" and I appreciate that you were able to give real life contradictions to their cynical beliefs that it is now always the worst of times, but it may have been a good idea to allow some of the other students to provide opposites or contradictions to all the "worst of times" concepts. Keeps them actively thinking and engaged.

6. Allowing the class to speak freely without needing to raise their hands does facilitate a nice and open discussion between the students and yourself. While in your classroom it began going well, but by the end the class had taken the floor away from you. Make sure to always redirect the discussion back to your focal point instead of allowing kids to spend the entire class period discussing with each other.

Here is Hunter College student Rifath Islam's take on Principal Clarke's "state-of-the-school" welcome speech to the Calvin Coolidge High School faculty in UP THE DOWN STAIRCASE:

The success of a school is measured in various different ways. While I was in high school, the Department of Education would do annual rounds in my school to check the statistics (graduation rate), the types of extracurriculars offered, how satisfied students were, etc. Depending on what each representative saw, the school would receive a rating, but naturally, there would be people who agreed and disagreed with the rating – most often, the student disagreed with the high ratings the school received. That being said, the principal will almost always take pride in their school, claiming it to be something of a great academy that preps students for a future like no other school can, but it doesn't always mean that they're right.

Principal Clarke is one of those principals who takes great pride in the success of his school, claiming that they follow a set of rules that ultimately best preps their students. In some ways, people would disagree with his statement, mainly if they're looking at the rate at which students at Calvin Coolidge High School dropped out. If this were the sole determining factor of how "well prepped" the school prepares its students, then perhaps the answer would be not well at all, for many students do not even stay. However, having gotten to know the students, specifically Miss Sylvia Barrett's students, I think the answer is quite the opposite and Calvin Coolidge does a dandy job at prepping its students.

From the beginning of Kaufman's novel, it was shown that many of the students did not do their work in Barrett's classroom, but the reason why could be attributed to the fact that many of the students were dealing with night jobs outside of school hours. At first glance, many of Miss Barrett's students could be made out to be insubordinate, but throughout the novel, through their written assignments and suggestion box notes, it is clear that many of the students are actually quite intelligent and many feel as though they are limited by teachers who don't really seem to care for them all that much. That being said, I would probably say that Principal Clarke is correct in saying that CCHS does well in prepping their students, but credit cannot be taken by the principal or the whole staff of teachers, but rather singular teachers here and there who make it clear to their students that their education and safety is a priority. After all, they say that under proper care, a student can blossom wonderfully.

And here is Rifath Islam's take on the choice of UP THE DOWN STAIRCASE as the title of Bel Kaufman's novel:

To Bel Kaufman,

Initially, having read the title of the novel, I was a little bit confused at what the title meant. The first thought that popped into my brain was a book I had read when I was younger, called WAYSIDE SCHOOL, that had all kinds of odd rules like having a designated up staircase and a designated down staircase (alongside designated up/down elevators). Naturally, this is what I had assumed the title of the book meant – and to and behold, I was correct!

Having gotten through to the end of the novel now, I think the title you have chosen for the novel is just the perfect fit – as compared to the previous title "From a Teacher's Wastebasket" for your short story. I think it was a very clever move of yours to name the novel as such, as it does not give anything away to the reader but rather makes them question what could the title possibly mean.

Miss Barrett considered leaving Calvin Coolidge High School altogether, as the frustration of all the moments in the school has mounted up and she seems to be at odds and ends. Ultimately, she decides to stay when she realizes that despite the struggles she's been facing in the classroom, she has been helping the students in some way or another and they, in fact, want her presence back at the school.

The title that you chose just perfectly wraps up the essence of the novel – the odd rules that the school implements and the insufferable number of memos that are constantly sent out throughout the school days. In naming the novel after the one memo that has Miss Barrett questioning her position at CCHS, you have managed to capture the entirety of the novel within four short but eye-catching words.

SESSION #28 OF THE TEACHER AND STUDENT IN LITERATURE ON THE MOST REMARKABLE FICTIONAL TEACHER AND MENTOR OF THE FALL 2020 COURSE

Dear Colleagues,

I hope it has been for you as exhausting (I worked you quite hard, I believe) and exhilarating (you rose to the occasion both intellectually and imaginatively, I know) as it has been for me in this first-time-ever remote edition of The Teacher and Student in Literature course. As I have not kept it a secret, you know that I truly missed getting to know you personally and professionally and to collegially learn from you "live"; maybe, for you lower-termers in the course, we can have that more direct collegial experience in the future in one of the other special topics courses I offer in the English Department: Some Day: The Literature of Waiting (English 25146) and Playing Detective (English 25145).

There is an old teacher joke that goes something like this (the joke, not the teacher, is old): A fairly new teacher is sitting around the Thanksgiving dinner table with several adult siblings (exclusively male. Her (or his) siblings are talking about what they make in their chosen professions (have you already inferred that they talk totally in monetary terms knowing that teachers in the United States are grossly under appreciated financially?). One of the siblings turns to the only teacher at the table and bluntly and condescendingly asks (in this psychological mind game that some successful professionals play), "What do *you* make?"

And the teacher responds (in what I believe is the winning move of the game):

"I make a difference."

In this connection and as a preparation for your last CW/HW of the course (due tonight to both Mr. Eidelberg and your course partner), let me share with you an excerpt from Daniel Mendelsohn's superb 2017 non-fiction book AN ODYSSEY: A FATHER, A SON, AND AN EPIC in which Mendelsohn, a college humanities professor, writes about how he taught a course on Homer's epic poem "The Odyssey" to a seminar class of undergraduates that included, as a senior citizen auditor, his elderly father:

> One of the strange things about teaching is that you can never know what the effect will be on others; can never know, if you have something to teach, who your real students will be, the ones who will take what you have to give and make it their own – "what you have to give" being, in no small part, what you yourself learned from some other teacher, someone who wondered whether you would absorb what she had to give, someone who is, by the time you're old enough to write about the experience, as old as your parents, perhaps even dead - can never really know which of the young people clustered around the seminar table is someone whom the teacher or the text has touched so deeply, for whatever reason, that the lesson will live beyond the classroom, beyond you.

> But then, the process of education, of pedagogy, *of leading a child into knowledge*, is a delicate and unpredictable one, its mechanism and effects often mysterious to a student and teacher alike.

> For instance:

> On the mild day in mid-May when Classics 125: The Odyssey of Homer ended, I was convinced that this experiment - having my father sit in on the seminar, an idea that so many of my and my parents friends had found so charming, so amusing - had borne no fruit.

Note how Mendelsohn reminds us that there can be no learning without teaching (two sides of the same educational "coin") because "education" (originally from the Latin language) literally means "a leading out from," as the teacher, primarily through carefully phrased focusing questions, helps the student to critically think about something, looking for patterns of meaning and make-sense connections in his or her factual knowledge base.

CW/HW

Think back over all the fictional teachers (both major and minor characters) you have come to meet this term in our course's novels novellas, short stories, feature films, excerpts from films, movie trailers, and chapters from Mr. Eidelberg's two texts, SO YOU THINK YOU MIGHT LIKE TO TEACH and STAYING AFTER SCHOOL.

Choose one such teacher to write a **personal letter** to (the voice, the vocabulary, and the content are all yours) in which you tell this fictional teacher how and why "meeting him or her in literature" has made "a difference" in your actual current life (as a human being, as a reader of serious literature, as a college student majoring in whatever and minoring in whatever, as a future teacher (or future member of another profession), as a member (or not) of a particular religion, as a member (or not) of a particular political party, as a New Yorker, as an immigrant or a child of immigrants, as an American-born citizen - you get the idea, right?

None of the sixteen students in the course chose as their favorite fictional teacher Muriel Spark's Jean Brodie, neither in or out of her prime. A discussion about that could be a whole other bonus session!

Here is Hunter College student Shelly Uzagir on her choice of Rick Dadier of the novel THE BLACKBOARD JUNGLE as fictional teacher of the course:

> Dear Richard Dadier,
>
> I was introduced to numerous teachers throughout this semester, in literature and film. Each person enlightened me with significant lessons for teaching. For example, Mark Thackeray taught me the importance of reminding (and convincing) students of their potential and ability to grow into well-mannered, educated and self-valued adults. Sylvia Barrett taught me there are school administrations that are concerned more with forms and rules rather than educating their students. However, with patience and care, a teacher can achieve their ultimate goal, to prepare their students for adulthood. However, I compared and contrasted each teacher I met to you, because

you made an impact on my life. I'm sure the organization of the introductions played a part – being that I met you first and you exposed the truth about teaching before anyone else. However, your teaching experience is unique. You were viewed as a hero and an enemy before you were viewed as a teacher. You changed my perspective on teaching because you showed me that you can receive the job, you can demand students refer to you as "Mrs." or "Mr.," you can even develop your own lesson plan, but you aren't a teacher until the students accept and acknowledge you as such.

Mr. Dadier, you worked tirelessly to earn the trust and respect of your students. It certainly wasn't easy, but I'm sure when you received that acceptance (and/or when Gregory Miller stood up for you), it felt rewarding. To be honest, I would've likely quit after getting jumped, almost losing my marriage, being falsely accused, receiving persecution for a heroic and moral act and, of course, having to avoid a stabbing or two. However, you knew you had a job to do and had no intention of giving up on your students. As a human, you taught me to be resilient. As a student, you taught me to be appreciative. As a (not American-born) citizen residing in a country where schools in low-income neighborhoods are used as a "keep-kids-off-the-streets" institution, you taught me to be hopeful that teachers like you exist in neighborhoods like mine.

It was a pleasure to meet you. I hope to hear from you again.

Sincerely,

Shelly Uzagir

Here is Hunter College student Jasmine Baird on her choice of Mark Thackeray of the feature film "To Sir, With Love" as fictional teacher of the course:

Dear Mr. Mark Thackeray,

I admire your courage in the feature film "To Sir, With Love" with you stepping out of your comfort zone by teaching at a school where the students feel everyone has given up on them, so therefore they act out. A lot of people do not have that type of patience. You were given a warning on your first day as a teacher that your class wasn't going to be an easy crowd but you still made sure to stick it out in the long run.

Teaching is not what you originally wanted to do – it was to be a civil engineer – yet you still managed to do a very good job. Where would your students be without you teaching them manners and basic life skills that are just as important as their school work. Honestly, I'm not too sure about the career path I will choose but I know that when I do, I want to be just as determined and forthcoming as you are. I'm currently majoring in sociology and minoring in English at Hunter College and I did not think in high school that I would've ended up in Hunter, but I'm glad that I did not give up because if I did then I wouldn't have been able to experience certain classes. I've always admired people who have ambition and I will keep striving in order to one day reach my goals.

Sincerely,

Jasmine Baird

Here is Hunter College student Jessica Ulloa on her choice of Mr. Chips of the novella GOODBYE, MR. CHIPS as fictional teacher of the course:

Dear Mr. Chips,

Reading the novella GOODBYE, MR. CHIPS has really shaped the way I see many things in a lot of areas that are not limited to being in the classroom. I read this heart-wrenching book as a recollection of your memory and of the mark you left on others. It truly shows how much you did for everyone, and that was incredibly beautiful to see. The storyline in general was very moving to see as you progressed in your life till the very end. My heart got so warm reading about you and your wife Katherine and your story made me relate several points to my partner, in ways that I myself learn from them as you did from your wife. The idea of you becoming a better person and absorbing things around you is a quality that is very incredible to have.

This has made me see and appreciate how much your students and people around you can move you to change your ways of thinking. It has helped me understand that gentleness is also something essential and important to have not only as an educator but just as a person in general. Meeting you has made me able to relate to myself somewhat, as I can be closed off and hard to know at first but open once I get to know someone.

It was nice to get a refreshing view on how people shaped and moved you as a person. Seeing your students and other educators love the way you thought made me feel very good. And at the end of the day this is the feeling of knowing that you made a difference and moved someone, or several people.

The way your story was written in flashbacks is also something I have always enjoyed and made me want to keep reading and being invested. Another part that overall moved me was the storyline of Katherine and how you met her and fell in love while on the trip to the Lake district of England. It was heartwarming to see how she helped you become more open and friendly with many people and helped you reach your goal of becoming the schoolmaster.

Best,

Jessica

Here is Hunter College student Khadiza Sultana on her choice of Frank McCourt of the novelized memoir TEACHER MAN as fictional teacher of the course:

Dear Mr. McCourt,

One of my life mottos is to be passionate about the things I set out to do. Whether that's learning how to play piano from YouTube, managing more than one extracurricular, or creating slideshows, as long as I'm passionate about something, I'm going to keep going because it makes me happy. My second life motto is to fake it till you make it; set out to be the livelier version of yourself, so much so that eventually you become comfortable in expressing yourself that way in front of others, even if the initial thought of meeting new people makes you nervous. For a while I had considered becoming an English teacher, but at some point I started having doubts. Even if I was passionate about the subject, would I prove to be a good teacher? Could I get past these worries and become the ideal teacher I want to be? In meeting you, I saw an older version of myself who didn't let her doubts get in the way. I saw someone who reaffirmed my beliefs, someone who could invigorate others by making themselves out to be the most eager to learn in a classroom, someone who wanted to teach with both passion and mastery. I saw someone who was trying to find their voice and learning to be comfortable in a classroom, something I wondered whether I was capable of doing as a teacher's assistant in senior year of high school. I met someone who gave me the advice I really needed and for that I'm thankful for our encounter.

You made teaching look so easy, but I know it wasn't all rainbows and sunshine for you. I appreciated the things you said on the subject of writing really well. So I want to start writing creatively again in my free time. I want to write out the stories I have in my head and become a better writer because I want to be better and because the end result makes me happy. I want to try a little more before deciding whether or not teaching is right for me. Like you said, maybe I might not achieve complete freedom, but I can try to drive fear into a corner. No matter what career field I decide on, I'm bound to have doubts and face struggles. But as long as I strive to improve so that I meet my Broadway audience halfway, as long as I grit my teeth and do the things I'm scared of doing, I'll be fine. So, thank you for re-awakening my interests and being a guide for the current me who's trying to figure things out.

Warmly,

Khadiza Sultana

Here is Hunter College student Mahajabin Chowdhury on her choice of Frank McCourt of the novelized memoir TEACHER MAN as fictional teacher of the course:

Dear Mr. Frank McCourt,

I have always felt school was important because it was a learning environment for students to gain an education, but you have made me realize going to school is one of many learning experiences in both a student and teacher's life. In your memoir, you described how you learned from your experience as a teacher. You were able to figure out what teaching style suits you and your students. It was remarkable how honest you were with your students that you and they would teach and grow. It reminds me how sometimes during a lesson a teacher will bring up his opinion during a discussion.

From my experience, I was never expected to automatically agree with his points, but rather I would be given the chance to present my thinking. Neither the students nor teachers would be wrong, but we do learn from each other's different points of view. I value a teacher's opinion based on how they value mine, so you have deeply established the respect you have towards your students. It was admirable how you find importance in the children learning rather than the material being taught. You have taught me that as a student to trust the way a teacher is teaching, as long as I am able to comprehend the information.

I have to commend your demeanor towards your students because of how much care you show them with no hesitation. You do not judge them for who they are or who their parents might be. You acknowledge their progress and how they learn in the classroom despite problems they might have outside the school environment. Mr. McCourt, I really respected how extensively seriously you took your role as a teacher. You did not just give content for them to learn, you gave them encouragement to follow their hopes and wishes.

In my life, I want to now value the time of the teachers who take their time and put in so much effort to get me to learn and engage during the lesson. I feel the best way to show my respect would be to participate in the discussions more often. Outside of school, I hope to now become mindful about what my parents or other family members have to say to me. When I do not agree with them, I should be able to explain why without a snide remark or any form of disrespect. Most importantly, you have taught me that my voice and opinions do matter, and nobody should have the power to tell me my thoughts are insignificant.

I am still not sure if I want to be a teacher in the professional world, but that should not prevent me from being a mentor and advising people when they are faced with an obstacle. I have three younger sisters, and I have learned how much they can learn from me, as I can learn from them too. It should not be considered embarrassing or outlandish because there are things they have experienced that I may not have, and vice versa. I hope to not just stop with my siblings but with other people I meet as I grow older.

Thank you, Mr. McCourt, for the lessons you have provided on your journey as a teacher.

Sincerely,

Mahajabin Chowdhury

Here is Hunter College student Hudaiba Khari on her choice of Mr. Parkhill of the novel THE EDUCATION OF HYMAN KAPLAN as fictional teacher of the course:

Dear Mr. Parkhill,

Meeting you in literature has been nothing but inspiring. I am very thankful to have the opportunity to have met you and learn from you about how to better myself. I admire your work ethic, determination, patience and kindness that you offer to your students. Prior to this semester or even mid-semester, I knew I wanted to pursue education but I was unclear what grade level I wanted this to be at. Teaching high school would mean more comprehension on the student side but I was still very lost. Reading about your patience and the impact you were able to create at the American Night Preparatory School for Adults inspired me to focus more on what is deeper within my heart. I decided to think more about what my purpose was for teaching and that was to genuinely make a difference. For me personally, I discovered that this was through teaching at elementary-level students. These students are young, bright and oftentimes given bad training, which translates to students in the future who hate education. I want to be part of the group that does the opposite, to project and help transfuse my love for education to the students I teach.

Thank you for helping me get back to the purpose I started with when it came to the teaching profession. One thing that I admired most about you is your persistent patience, especially with students like Hyman Kaplan. I thought teaching adults in particular would mean that it would be easy, but reading about your classroom proved me wrong. You were incredibly patient with all your students and it was clear that you taught with impartiality. You were consistent with your manners and, despite how you felt, you made sure your response was of candor. I think this is a skill that I need to master and I would like to perfect. While I do have a high threshold of becoming annoyed at a person, I would like to improve that further and ensure that I show everyone the love (maybe to a lower extent) that I give to my loved ones.

It takes skill to be truthful, yet kind, helpful and generous, and I believe you, sir, have done an exceptional job at that. I commend you and hope to learn to do the same. From the perspective of a practicing Muslim, you also have highlighted the importance of enthusiasm and love for a goal or desire. For you, I saw it through your teaching and the students' excitement that they had in your class. For me, I want to work towards more specific things that I set my mind to. I want to focus more on my religion and return to the pure dedication and reward that I received from it. I think it was a happier me and it is worth the effort to go back.

Overall, I wanted to give a sincere thank you for everything you have taught me and the progress you helped the students make and the support you have given them constantly. Your profession is not an easy one, and I would like to remind you that you are doing a great job. You are kind, loving, and great at what you do. Please continue to do so. Thank you again for your service and making a difference. I hope to do the same.

Best regards and a warm thank you,

Hudaiba Khatri

Here is Hunter College student Janel Fernandez on her choice of Mr. Parkhill of the novel THE EDUCATION OF HYMAN KAPLAN as fictional teacher of the course:

Dear Mr. Parkhill,

I read a small excerpt from Daniel Mendelsohn's non-fiction book AN ODYSSEY: A FATHER, A SON, AND AN EPIC, which was shared with me by a Hunter College professor named Robert Eidelberg. "One of the strangest things about teaching is that you can never know what your effect will be on others... who your real students will be, the ones who will take what you have to give and make it their own." Although I was no student in your classroom, I have taken what you gave me and made my own of it. You have made a difference in my current life as a future teacher and student. Talk about patience, love and dedication, you are such a respectful, kind-hearted, and a mild-mannered teacher. It was an honor meeting you (but not really meeting you) in Leonard Q. Ross's book THE EDUCATION OF HYMAN KAPLAN.

"Watching" you teach at the American Night Preparatory School for Adults was so inviting. The students in your class are all different from those that have been introduced to me throughout the observations of other classrooms. Although the students in your class have no patience for one another – I'm assuming because they are much older, and become frustrated with one particular student more than others (Kaplan) – they never ever disrespected you and they never doubted your corrections or suggestions. They looked up to you; they praised you.

You are a very dedicated teacher, you always find a way to connect with your students. I'm a teacher as well. I don't teach adults, I teach little ones, which also requires a lot of patience, love, and understanding. I hope to bring all that you bring to your students to mine. I hope that as they grow they remember how much of a kind teacher I was to them. Most importantly how much I care, and how much I respect them and their success.

Both of my parents are immigrants. My father was born and raised in the Dominican Republic. He arrived in the United States at the age of fourteen. My mother was born in Ecuador and arrived when she was fifteen years old. I helped my mother study for her citizenship exam last year. Happy to announce she passed it. I was born and raised in the United States. I learned the history of our country at a very young age. Knowing why there are 50 stars on the American flag is such a norm for me. So to ask my mom the questions for this exam and her response to me being "I have no idea, for looks?" made me laugh but also made me realize that there are a lot of immigrants who come here for a better education and a better living. To provide for their family.

The United States this year has seen a deadly pandemic, a global movement for racial justice, and ICE raids like no other. So to watch you give your all to these students who probably come from nothing and wake up every morning to be better and do better has changed me as a teacher, student, daughter of immigrants and as a human being in what can be a cruel world.

All the very best,

Janel Fernandez

P.S. Share this with Professor Eidelberg. I wouldn't have "met" you without him. Let him know I said THANK YOU! Thank you for believing in all his students, and that absolutely every session pushed me to the very end.

Here is Hunter College student Victoria Cecere on her choice of Sylvia Barrett of the novel UP THE DOWN STAIRCASE as fictional teacher of the course:

Dear Miss Sylvia Barrett,

In my Teacher and Student in Literature class, we were told to write to one of the teachers we've learned about through our course this semester. I decided to write to you. I must say, I was surprised by how much I related to you and enjoyed your story. However, there was a lot of competition. From Richard Dadier, one who also wanted to make a difference with his students, to Miss Jean Brodie, a woman who was just as obsessed with her prime as she was in being a person that her followers could adore. Though both teachers did intrigue me, I realized that your story had affected me the most.

I started with the idea that we had experienced similar things. UP THE DOWN STAIRCASE made so much sense, especially considering that you had literally and physically gone up the down staircase and felt a bit "stuck." That is a feeling I still struggle with, though I no longer have to worry about physically going up the wrong staircase. But, as an "almost" education major, I realize that all people suffer from a small dose of imposter syndrome. I think it comes with the coming of age, specifically because people are told that they have to have all of their ducks in a row as soon as *humanly possible* to avoid being judged by others. Whether it was meant or not, I saw a bit of that in you too. There was the fear of not being able to adapt to your teaching position, and not being able to teach your students anything. It affected you and luckily made you strive to do better. Unfortunately, that doesn't happen to everyone. Though I wish it did make others strive to do more, many would have quit that first day or during that first week. However, you managed to tough it out and I give you credit for that. I wish I had read your story during my teaching internship, it would have helped me quite a bit. Though our situations weren't completely similar, it would have helped me hold my head high knowing that I was trying my hardest. I also appreciated learning about the difference you make in your students' lives. Although I haven't had such a breakthrough yet, the "student" I've had the longest, my younger sister Emily, did inform me that I've make a difference in her life. That gave me the confidence boost I needed to continue my studies. I want to be a teacher that makes a difference, even if it's one that is very small. After all, a little goes a long way. You've helped me realize that it's okay to struggle or feel as though your efforts are not being received correctly. But instead, when I do feel like I need to work harder, I need to try to get my point across the right way.

When thinking about the prompt, as well as the teaching joke attached, I realized that teachers do make a difference, yourself included. After all, they don't get paid as much as they should, as seen in my previous rants about the way educators are paid despite their hard work and service to both schools and the community. However, it's more ironic to know that without teachers at all levels, doctors would not be able to get the certification needed to start assisting medically. It's true! That teacher in the old teacher's joke is right when they say that they make a difference. For some, it could be the difference between a person getting their doctorate or starting an MLM scheme. I'm completely kidding about the one, but the point remains. Without teachers, there wouldn't be a way for doctors to get to the point they want to be at. Instead, we would have to change the rate of pay for each profession to accurately represent qualifications. Qualifications would be minimal if they existed at all. In all, a world without teaches would be a very terrible place, especially when considering the job market and advanced opportunities. In thinking about this prompt as well as the joke, I realized that you were one of the teachers that had a significant impact in such a short amount of time. It was almost impressive, disregarding your visit to the hospital, of course. Your impact made me look at myself, it made me try to evaluate what I wanted to accomplish in life. I realized that I wanted to have an effect similar to yours, one that could help my students even if they were struggling. In doing so, I realized that general teaching might not be the best avenue for me and my pursuits. Instead, I may need to evaluate my options a bit more. I think I may specialize in something, something that can help me make it difference. Be it special ed or TESOL, I've realized that I would not have enough to bring to the metaphorical table. But I need to learn my place there. You made me realize that no matter what you do - or where you come from - what's important is what you do each day to better yourself and your situation. That is something I will always take with me as I try to navigate both college and my future career. Though I wish I could write more I know that I have other responsibilities to take care of. Unfortunately, my spring semester is not finished just yet. However, I'd like to end this letter by thanking you so much for continuing to teach even when you felt like you had been beaten. There is so much to learn from that portion of your story alone, as shows that you sometimes have to deal with the cards that you're given. I hope the novel has a sequel! I would love to know how your story continued. Either way I wish you the best.

With appreciation,

Victoria Cecere

Here is Hunter College student Anika Bradley on her choice of two (2!) secondary character teachers as her fictional teachers of the course. That's right, neither choice is the major character in their respective novel (from the "bookend" novels of The Teacher and Student in Literature course – UP THE DOWN STAIRCASE at the end and THE BLACKBOARD JUNGLE at the start). By way of explanation, Anika began her assignment with this note:

Hi Prof. Eidelberg!

Attached as a Word document is my response to the CW/HW for the final session of our course on The Teacher and Student in Literature. I hope you don't mind but I wrote two letters instead of one. I just had two teachers I felt strongly about, and their stories were too different to choose just one. Please let me know if you have any questions or concerns, and I hope you enjoy them!

Dear Mrs. Bea Schachter,

I've met a lot of different kinds of teachers this semester in a course I'm taking in college, but you've offered up a perspective and a teaching persona that I would most like to be someday.

I went to a large, overcrowded, inner-city high school in Chicago and while the feeling of sheer chaos that I experienced with Sylvia Barrett was definitely an interesting, somewhat realistic one, your experience was a realistic one too! I imagine you being a lot like Sylvia on your first day at Calvin Coolidge (or whatever other high school you started at) and I hope you had someone like yourself in your corner on that day. After the first twelve pages of strictly dialogue from Sylvia's first homeroom period, the next piece of paper we see, as readers and as Sylvia, is an encouraging message from you! Letting her know that even in the midst of a hellish first day, she had a friend there for her who's been in her shoes and has her back!

That really stood out to me because you're living a good like at Calvin Coolidge at this point in your career - teaching kids who want to learn and teaching lessons you want to teach, but you've still decided to take that extra step and be there for a fellow first-time teacher and for all your students! The Calvin Coolidge Clarion is definitely the most interesting and hectic piece of school newspaper I've ever seen, and I loved every word of it! But especially the teacher's superlatives. It's the first time we're introduced to the student's perspective of you and even then, they think of you as "the teacher readiest with unselfish help" and call you the "mom" of the school! Though it's the first time, it is definitely not the last time a student mentions they thought they have never had you but heard that you genuinely care about the students here, like Sylvia. You have a reputation for just being a kind and good person and I think that's beautiful!

Teaching is not an easy job, especially in an overcrowded and underfunded school like yours, but I believe you're doing exactly what you set out to do - to make a difference. You are completely aware that your school is not the best environment for learning but that's exactly why you stay, and you told Sylvia as much! You are needed in that place and you know that you can help more kids at CC than you can ever help in college or some fancy private school. Sure, they might have window poles, textbooks, and a working custodian, but that's not what matters and you know it. As long as your classroom has an open door policy (that is NOT out of order) and you are doing what you can to help the future adults of tomorrow, then you know you're doing your best and I love that. I want to take from your book when I enter my first teaching job, because I love your creative style and open arms attitude in the best and worst of environments.

So, of all the teachers I've studied this semester, you had the most positive and awe-inspiring effect on me!

Sincerely,

Anika Bradley

Dear Mr. Joshua Edwards,

When I first met you in THE BLACKBOARD JUNGLE, I immediately fell in love with your character. One of the first times we see you is when you're practically bursting with excitement over having your own classroom at your first teaching job.

Rick Dadier was an okay character, but my course partner and I both agreed we connected with you right away because of your sheer enthusiasm and joy. As I was reading that scene, I truly *felt* every inch of your excitement over having that one classroom that's all yours to teach in all year! Seeing you act like that and not being able to keep it together when talking to Rick made me feel your giddy attitude as well!

I've read a lot of different stories about a lot of different teachers this semester, but yours felt like one of the most tragic to me. You're so pure and to watch you fall into despair when you were trying your hardest was a sad thing to witness. I wish I could know where you are now, and what you're doing. I hope you went back to teaching and gave it another shot. It's so clear how much you care and I was crushed when you quit.

We watched Rick fall into mind games and manipulations with some of his students and take the path of deciding to be the "tough guy" and pretend he's not the person he truly is, and I admired you more for never doing that. It's one thing to put on a "teacher persona" to be able to wrangle your class into learning a thing or two, but you shouldn't lose sight of everything you are, and what you are is genuine.

Before writing this letter, I wrote a letter to high school writing teacher Mrs. Beatrice Schachter, and she reminds me a lot of you. Her story, to me at least, looks a lot like how I would imagine your happy ending, an ending I hope you find someplace one day. I learned so much from the both of you this semester (even though neither of you were the main characters of your novels!).

From Bea, I learned that taking up space in your own life and creating a positive reputation for yourself by never giving up and continuing to care (even when it feels impossible) is extremely important, and things might get a little easier one day. But from you, Joshua, I learned the importance of working in and finding a school you can find your place in. Maybe Rick's faux-tough guy persona made him more cut out for such a rough and tumble environment, maybe that's something that would just never work for you because that's truly not who you are. But you'll find a place you can belong in, I know.

I wish you could write me back if you needed to. I never want you to completely lose the enthusiasm you inspired in me at the beginning of your story. I wish I could actually tell you that

I'm here to talk if you want because I believe in you. I know you can do this, you've worked too hard to give up now. So here's hoping your character is out there somewhere doing great things!

Sincerely,

Anika Bradley

Here is Hunter College Student Martin Ljuljduraj on his choice of Rick Dadier of the novel THE BLACKBOARD JUNGLE as fictional teacher of the course – along with a postscripted shout out to the factual teacher of the course.

Dear Rick Dader,

I just wanted to take some time to express how much I enjoyed meeting you at North Manuel Trades High School in the novel THE BLACKBOARD JUNGLE written by "your" author Evan Hunter. There is no other teacher that comes to mind who could have made more of a difference than you have in my actual current life as a human being. You see, I have been a student all of my life and will be until the day I die and that is undeniable. The reason, however, as to why I say that you've made such an impact is you were consistent, smart, and most importantly caring with your students. I have had the privilege of having real in-person classes with real and *live* teachers. The difference between those teachers and yourself, you might ask, is that I have never met you nor will I ever have the opportunity to do so because you are a fictional character made up to be used in this book and later used in the movie based off the book. You were stern and yet fair with your students and these two qualities alone are, I believe, among the most important that every teacher currently existing needs to pick up from you. In addition, you found the time to talk to all your students in your English class individually and that isn't a common practice seen much in the high school years I have been blessed to experience. And to top all of it off, you taught the most realistic lessons. What I mean by this is you always related the lessons to real-life examples that would allow the material to make more logical sense to students and always gave them something to relate the lessons to. You have done everything that a teacher could humanly do for your students and that is something which is truly special even though I am reading all of it in black and white. It has been a pleasure meeting you without seeing you in person.

Best regards,

Martin Ljuljduraj

P.S. When you get a chance, hand this letter to a professor named Robert Eidelberg. This is actually for him, please. And thank you.

KUDOS FROM STUDENTS IN THE ONLINE COURSE OF THE TEACHER AND STUDENT IN LITERATURE

Thank you for everything you have done for us this semester. Though, yes, The Teacher and Student in Literature has been a bit of a challenge with the course load, it has been a fun ride! I've never attended a class that was so diverse in the way that yours was. You opened us up to prompts that pushed us to stand in the shoes of characters that we would have otherwise just simply analyzed for the sake of the work, and you pushed us to adopt a different way of thinking when it came to literature. By no means was this semester easy, with all the challenges remote learning had to offer, but you handled it well and created a teaching method that kept students both engaged and up to date. It has been an honor having you as our course instructor this semester and I loved everything this course had to offer!

-- Rifath Islam, Hunter College upper sophomore

Thank you so much for a great semester! I really enjoyed the class and most of the novels a lot! The creative writing prompts were always super inspiring and fun, especially doing the "in-voice" writings. You've been a great professor and thank you again for everything.

-- Anika Bradley, Hunter College lower sophomore

Professor, I chose this class as an elective because I enjoy writing. Although it was a challenge at times, the literature, the prompts, the creative writing assignments were all thought-provoking and enjoyable. Teaching is not the career path for me, but this course taught me so much about the experience, the school system, and the unfortunate circumstances of students. I'm thankful for all that I've learned.

-- Shelly Uzagir, Hunter College upper junior

Professor Eidelberg, thank you for the knowledge, the creative writing assignments, and critical thinking prompts. They were all a challenge, and the teacher and student novels we read were all so good – some more than others – but I am still so very grateful to be able to add them to my library collection. And to my course partner Martin Ljuljduraj, I can't thank you enough for your patience and understanding whenever I needed guidance.

-- Janel Fernandez, Hunter College upper junior

Even though it was through email and I never got to meet you, Professor, I felt a sort of camaraderie between you and my course partner Janel Fernandez and me all the way through the course. From the way you wrote the assignments, I could see that you cared about what you assigned as homework, especially the required pieces of creative writing. They were something I had never done before, and I hope that I did a good job on them.

-- Martin Ljuljduraj, Hunter College upper sophomore

Thank you, Professor, for an amazing semester. Professor, your prompts have really strengthened my creative writing abilities. And thank you, my course partner, Victoria Cecere, it was a privilege to be able to read and be inspired by all your writing.

-- Destiny Bolding, Hunter College upper sophomore

Thank you so much, Professor, for the wonderful semester! It has been a pleasure. I am so grateful that I got to take the course, and I hope that I have you again. And to my course partner, Destiny Bolding, thank you for all the help and hard work. I enjoyed working with you and hope we have some classes together in the future on campus.

-- Victoria Cecere, Hunter College upper freshman

AUTHOR/EDITOR ROBERT EIDELBERG'S BOOKS WITH A BUILT-IN TEACHER

In addition to *The Teacher and Student in Literature: A Literature Study and Creative Writing Course to TAKE or to TEACH*, the following Books With a Built-in Teacher by educator, author and editor Robert Eidelberg are available through all online booksellers as well as from the author through his email address glamor62945@mypacks.net

Evidently, My Dear Armchair Detective: Solving Ten Classic Mysteries Together With Their Celebrated Sleuths

Hey, Professor: An Experiment in Distance Learning and Teaching

Some Day: The Literature of Waiting – A Creative Writing Course With Time on Its Hands

"Who's There?" in Shakespeare's HAMLET - That Is the Question!

Stanza-Phobia: A Self-Improvement Approach to Bridging Any Disconnect Between You and Poetry by Understanding Just One Poem (Yes, One!) and Winding Up Not Only Learning the Process Involved but Coming to Love at Least a Few More Poems (and Maybe Poetry itself)

Good Thinking: A Self-Improvement Approach to Getting Your Mind to Go from "Huh?" to "Hmm" to "Aha!"

Playing Detective: A Self-Improvement Approach to Becoming a More Mindful Thinker, Reader, and Writer By Solving Mysteries

Detectives: Stories for Thinking, Solving, and Writing

So You Think You Might Like to Teach: 29 Fictional Teachers (for Real!) Model How to Become and Remain a Successful Teacher

Staying After School: 19 Students (for Real!) Have the Next What-if Word on Remarkable Fictional Teachers and Their Often Challenging Classes (a collaborative book based on the Hunter College course "The Teacher and Student In Literature")

Julio: A Brooklyn Boy Plays Detective to Find His Missing Father (with John Carter)

ABOUT EDUCATOR/AUTHOR
ROBERT EIDELBERG

A former print journalist, Robert Eidelberg served for thirty-two years as a secondary school teacher of English language arts and literature in the largest urban school system in the United States - the New York City school system - with nineteen and a half of those years as a teacher, an advisor, a supervising mentor, and the chair of the English Department and the Library Media Center of a highly diverse and 4,000-strong Queens neighborhood high school named after the poet and editor William Cullen Bryant.

For several years after that, Mr. Eidelberg was an editorial and educational consultant to Amsco, a foundational school publications company, as well as a writing instructor in several public and private community colleges and a student-teaching field supervisor and mentor in English education on the campus of Brooklyn College of the City University of New York under the auspices of the national Teaching Fellows Program.

For the past twenty-two years, Mr. Eidelberg has been a college adjunct in both the School of Education and in the English Department of Hunter College of the City University of New York. At Hunter College, Mr. Eidelberg currently offers three English Department special topics literature study and creative courses especially created for undergraduates either majoring or minoring in English, sociology, philosophy, psychology, history, and the sciences: The Teacher and Student in Literature, The Literature of Waiting, and Playing Detective.

As an author and editor, Mr. Eidelberg has published to date twelve intellectual-growth self-improvement books featuring his unique interactive "books with a built-in teacher" approach to close reading, critical thinking, and creative writing.

Robert Eidelberg lives in the historic Park Slope neighborhood of Brooklyn, New York, with his life partner of 48 years and their Whippet, Chandler, who, like his predecessor, Marlowe, is named in honor of the noir mystery writer Raymond Chandler.

CPSIA information can be obtained
at www.ICGtesting.com
Printed in the USA
FSHW010059310521
81887FS

9 781664 163744